SECRETS OF THE SEA

Published in association with National Sea Products Ltd.,
the producer of High Liner-branded fish products.

SECRETS OF THE SEA

THE FRESH APPEAL OF FROZEN FISH

ROSE MURRAY

Grosvenor House Press Inc.
Toronto – Montréal

The Publisher wishes to express its gratitude to

National Sea Products Ltd., the producer of High Liner-branded fish products, for its financial assistance in making the publication of this book possible.

Grosvenor House Press Inc.
111 Queen St. E.
Suite 456
Toronto, Ontario
M5C 1S2

Éditions Grosvenor Inc.
1456, rue Sherbrooke ouest
3e étage
Montréal (Quebec)
H3G 1K4

Canadian Cataloguing in Publication Data

Murray, Rose.
Secrets of the sea

ISBN 0-919959-42-3

1. Cookery (Fish). 2. Fish fillets.
I. Title. TX747.M87 1988
641.6'92 C88-095385-3

Design: Robert Torrans Associates Limited
Photography: Fred Bird & Associates
Food styling: Olga Truchan
Props co-ordination: Sandy Glud
Editor: Beverley Renahan
Printed and bound in Canada

On the cover:
Stir-fried Cod with Peppers and Cashews (page 58)
Sole Waves (page 14) and Raita Sauce (page 81)
Fish Salad Crécy (page 76)

CONTENTS

PREFACE

There's no question about it: seafood suits today's lifestyles. It's healthy, it's nutritious, it's low in calories, and it's delicious!

So why is it we Canadians eat so much less seafood than, say, Europeans? Partly because until the last ten to fifteen years it was difficult to get it, unless you lived on the east or west coast. Modern technology has done away with that problem. At National Sea, we freeze the fish we catch right where it's landed, so that, wherever you live in Canada, you can choose from a whole range of delicious products at your local store.

But I also believe there's another reason: most Canadians, not having a long European-style tradition of seafood cookery, don't know many great seafood recipes. That's a shame because there are so many different ways to serve wonderful seafood, ranging from the plain yet elegant to the sensationally fancy. Not to mention soups, chowders, appetizers and dips. It's to solve that problem that this book has been written. I hope you enjoy it, just as I'm sure you and your family will enjoy the delicious results!

> Gordon Cummings
> President and C.E.O.,
> National Sea Products, Halifax

NOTE:

National Sea Products, with its headquarters in Halifax, Nova Scotia, is the largest vertically integrated seafood company in North America. The company catches its own fish, operating a fleet of sea vessels, and markets fresh, frozen, and pre-cooked seafood throughout Canada and the United States. In Canada, look for famous High Liner brand frozen fillets, entrées and breaded products — wherever you shop.

INTRODUCTION

Even in land-locked areas of the country, eating fish is "in". Fish is pushing aside the meat-and-potatoes diet as more health-conscious Canadians learn that most fish contains less fat and fewer calories than meat and poultry.

But fish is more than just a trendy food. Besides its obvious health appeal as a low-fat, low-cholesterol source of high-quality protein, it has ease of preparation going for it in an age when people who have no time to cook constantly reach for convenience foods. Fish is, in fact, an original "fast" food that's particularly simple to cook.

Fish fillets are especially easy to use since there's no need to wrestle with scales, bones or any other part of the fish you don't need. For this reason too, fillets are economical. You throw away nothing and because they cook very quickly and have little fat, there's no shrinkage. Fillets, fresh-frozen when caught, have the added advantage of having no fishy taste or smell. And remember, not only is fresh-frozen fish as nutritious and flavorful as fresh fish, it is available year-round too.

Fish is fashionable because it is so versatile. Traditional chowders or old-fashioned fish and chips can be reassuring at a time when we need comfort foods. On the other hand, it can be upscale, sleek and sophisticated as the world moves ahead and people search for the new and the different.

Then, of course, there is the wonderful taste — enough to make any food stylish. The recipes that follow will convince you of fish's fabulous flavor as well as its convenience, ease, versatility, nutritional value and thriftiness.

Although *Secrets of the Sea* is not a diet book, the recipes were developed with a common-sense approach to the use of butter, oils, cream, salt and sugar. These are used in moderation while other flavor seasonings, such as herbs, spices, vegetables, fruits, wines and vinegars, are employed to enhance the taste of fish without distracting from its leanness and goodness.

Fresh herbs are more widely available these days but where not available, substitute about ⅓ the amount of dried for fresh.

The recipes in this book show both imperial and metric measures. Be sure to use one or the other throughout a recipe and not alternate between the two systems. For convenience of measuring, we have followed the Metric Commission Canada guidelines; equivalents are not necessarily identical to the imperial (for example, 1 lb is commonly adapted to metric as 500 g, when it really measures 454 g; 1 cup is adapted to metric as 250 mL, not 238 mL).

Handled and cooked properly, frozen fish brings to the table the roar of the surf and the closeness of the sea so as you cook through the book, you'll discover the fresh appeal of frozen fish.

Rose Murray

Rose Murray
Cambridge, Ont.

ALL ABOUT FROZEN FISH FILLETS

Buying and Storing

Fresh-freezing techniques and proper shipping guarantee the fresh flavor and good quality of today's fish even miles from the sea. To ensure this quality lasts until the fish is on your table, here are a few tips on buying and storing frozen fish fillets.

Dig down underneath the load line of the supermarket freezer case, and choose a clean package that is as hard as a rock and odor-free. Avoid any packages that have visible frost, or are misshappen or torn. The fillets themselves should be glossy with no dark spots, papery edges or discoloration.

Pick up frozen fish at the last minute in the supermarket, and don't allow it to sit in a hot car or to partially thaw. If you don't plan to use it immediately, store the fish in its original packaging in your home freezer at a temperature no higher than 0°F (−18°C). Because home freezers cannot keep fish as solidly frozen as commercial ones which have temperatures no higher than −15°F (−26°C), plan to use the fish as quickly as possible, but at any rate, store lean species, e.g., cod, sole, Boston bluefish, haddock, ocean perch, no longer than six months and fatty species, e.g., mackerel, arctic char, swordfish, halibut (medium-fat), turbot (medium-fat), no longer than three months.

Because of metric adaptation, 1 lb is commonly referred to in this book as 500 g. However, the common package size of frozen fish is 1 lb or 454 g, and all recipes have been developed using this package size of fish. Allow ¼ to ⅓ lb (125 to 175 g) fish per serving.

Thawing

In some recipes, such as those calling for poached fish or soups and stews, you can cook frozen fillets without thawing. However, thawing is recommended in recipes for breaded fish, fish cooked in a sauce, marinating, frying, broiling, barbecuing or microwaving. I also suggest rinsing the fish and patting or gently pressing it with paper towel until very dry before breading or dipping it in batter; coatings will not stick well to wet fish.

To thaw, place unopened package in a bowl and leave it, loosely covered, in the refrigerator overnight. Or place unopened package in cold water for 30 minutes to two hours. To partially thaw, refrigerate frozen package for two hours or place under cold running water for 10 minutes. To thaw in the microwave, place unopened package directly on oven floor and thaw on defrost cycle for 3 to 5 minutes per pound (500 g) in a 700-watt oven; turn package over halfway through. Or thaw one fillet for 1 to 2 minutes, turning once. Let package stand, unopened, for 5 minutes. (Check after minimum defrosting times; corners should not feel warm although outer pieces may start to loosen.) To free fish entirely of ice crystals, rinse under cold running water until fillets can be easily separated. (Thawing times depend upon the temperature of your freezer and how solidly frozen the fish is.)

Never thaw frozen fish at room temperature and never refreeze unused portions.

Cooking

Since fish is naturally tender, it benefits from short cooking times. Overcooking means fish will be rubbery, dry, mealy and depleted of its delicate flavor. Generally, it should be cooked for a short time at a high temperature.

Canada contributed greatly to fish cookery when the Department of Fisheries advised cooks to measure the depth of the fish (including stuffing) at its thickest point and to cook for 10 minutes per inch (5 to 7 minutes per cm). For partially thawed fish, add 1 to 2 minutes. For solidly frozen blocks of fish, increase the cooking time by half or double it; for individually frozen fillets, add 2 to 3 minutes. Times will depend on method of cooking and other ingredients in the recipe.

Be sure to test fish before the cooking time is up. During cooking, the flesh gradually turns from translucent to opaque. To test for doneness, place fork tines into fish at a 45-degree angle and twist: if fish resists and still has some translucency, then it is not done; if it flakes easily and is milky white, then it is just right.

Poaching gives delicate, moist results and is often used when fish is to be eaten cold in a salad or sandwich, used hot in a casserole or made into fish cakes, or served with a delicate sauce.

One pound (500 g) fish fillets will make about 2 cups (500 mL) flaked cooked fish.

Use just enough liquid (water, milk, stock, clam juice, wine or any combination) to cover fish. Add seasonings such as lemon slices, bay leaf, herbs, celery leaves or peppercorns. Bring liquid to a boil on top of stove, in oven or in microwave; immerse fish and simmer (without boiling or bubbling). Remove fish as soon as it is done. Strain the poaching liquid and use in sauces or soups. Poaching whole fillets takes 5 to 10 minutes if frozen, generally less time than baking (refer to the Canadian rule, above).

Steaming is another effective method of achieving delicate results without adding fat. Place fish in perforated steaming tray over lightly boiling water, wine or other liquid. Cover tightly and cook slightly longer than outlined in the Canadian rule (see this page).

Fillets may be steamed on a heatproof plate held above the boiling water with sealer rings or crumpled foil. Make sure the plate is at least 1 inch (2.5 cm) smaller in diameter than the pot.

Pan-frying is an excellent way to quickly cook fillets crispy on the outside without losing too much moisture. Coat thawed, well-dried fillets with seasoned flour or cornstarch (or dip floured fillets in milk and/or beaten egg, then in a coating such as bread crumbs, cracker crumbs, cornmeal, pancake mix, grated Parmesan cheese, chopped nuts, sesame seeds or a combination). The coating will adhere better if you refrigerate coated fillets for 30 to 60 minutes before cooking. Remember to shake off excess floury coatings before frying.

Melt butter with oil in a heavy skillet large enough to accommodate the fillets without crowding. Cook fillets, uncovered, over medium-low to medium heat for 1½ to 3 minutes per side or according to the Canadian rule (see this page).

Sautéing is tossing the fish — in a hotter pan than that used for pan-frying — over medium heat. Stir-frying is a form of sautéing, using bite-sized pieces of fish and cooking over high heat, usually in a wok.

Baking or **oven-frying** requires much less fat than pan-frying yet the fillets can achieve a crisp coating without drying out. Bake fish, uncovered, at 400-450°F (200-230°C) according to the Canadian rule (see this page). If baked in a sauce, add 5 minutes per inch (2.5 cm) thickness of fish. If the sauce contains cream, egg or cheese, reduce the temperature to 350°F (180°C) and increase the cooking time slightly.

Oven-steaming is used in the recipe for Sole and Vegetables Baked in Parchment (page 62). Season fish with lemon juice and/or herbs and wrap in foil or parchment paper. Place on baking sheet and bake at 425-450°F (220-230°C) according to the Canadian rule (page 10).

Deep-frying is the method used to achieve a very crisp, crunchy exterior on fillets that are breaded, batter-coated or dusted with seasoned cornmeal. For easy handling, cut large fillets into smaller pieces; keep batter and fish cold until just before cooking (cold batter absorbs less oil); crumb coatings adhere better if coated fish is refrigerated for 30 to 60 minutes before frying.

In a deep fryer or deep heavy saucepan, bring 3½ inches (9 cm) of oil (vegetable, peanut, safflower or corn) to 375°F (190°C) or until a 1-inch (2.5 cm) cube of white bread turns golden brown in 40 seconds. With tongs or frying basket (remember that batter-coated fillets may stick to the wire mesh), carefully lower a few pieces at a time into the hot fat; cook until golden brown, 3 to 4 minutes. Drain well on rack or crumpled paper towels; reheat the oil before cooking the next batch. Serve fish immediately. (If you store the oil for future fish-frying, cook a piece of potato in it to clear it; strain, cover and refrigerate.)

Broiling is a fast, simple method of sealing in the moisture and flavor of fish. You can vary the tastes by marinating or topping the fish just before broiling, or serving it with a flavored butter or sauce (see "Jazz It Up", page 79).

Arrange fish on greased preheated broiler pan, lined with foil for easier clean-up. Tuck any thin edges of fish under and brush with butter or oil, if not using a marinade or other topping. Broil 3 to 4 inches (8 to 10 cm) from heat (increase distance if cooking frozen fish) and cook according to the Canadian rule (page 10). Turn fish only if thicker than 1 inch (2.5 cm).

Barbecuing is an extremely quick cooking method with deliciously different results. If not overcooked, fillets will be very tender and succulent with a subtle smokiness that brings out their full flavor. For best results, fish should be just thawed, very cold and patted as dry as possible. (Very lean fillets benefit from marinating for 30 minutes or from using a basting sauce.) Place oiled fish directly on oiled grill or in oiled hinged grilling basket about 4 inches (10 cm) from medium-hot coals or at medium-high setting. Cook slightly less than outlined in the Canadian rule (page 10), turning only the thicker pieces with greased spatula or two.

Very fragile fillets, such as sole, can be cooked on a sheet of perforated oiled foil (see Tarragon-Lemon Sole, page 70). Make plenty of holes so the barbecue smoke can penetrate to flavor the fish. Total cooking time will vary according to the temperature, wind conditions and other variables associated with outdoor cooking.

Microwaving is a boon to small families and singles. For an incredibly easy individual serving, use the individually frozen fillets. Place a thawed fillet on a dinner plate; dot with butter if desired (fat is not necessary for microwaving). Drizzle with lemon juice; sprinkle with pepper, herbs and/or seasonings, such as paprika, dillweed, grated lemon rind, or spread with your choice of Flavored Butters (page 84). Cover with vented plastic wrap and microwave at High for 1 to 1½ minutes.

If microwaving 1 pound (500 g), arrange thawed fillets in a single layer with thickest parts toward the outside of a shallow dish, tucking under thin ends of fillets for even cooking. Cover with waxed paper or vented plastic wrap (depending on how much moisture you want retained) and microwave at High for 4 to 6 minutes, rotating dish and rearranging fillets halfway through cooking, until flesh is opaque and flakes easily when tested with a fork. Let stand, covered, for 3 minutes. Remember that although fish should be cooked all the way through, it will become rubbery, dry and tasteless if overcooked.

These cooking times were tested in a full-size 700-watt microwave oven. If your oven is different, cooking times may have to be adjusted.

Note: Fish must be completely thawed before microwaving; otherwise the edges of the frozen fish will be cooked when the centre is still cold.

SPECIES OF FISH

"There are more than 20,000 kinds of fish — as many as amphibians, reptiles, birds and mammals added together . . ." wrote Waverly Root in *Food*.

With such a wide variety to choose from, the novice cook may sometimes be confused about what kind to use. In this book, most of the fillets can be used interchangeably, but it is interesting to know why specific kinds have been suggested for certain recipes.

Texture plays a big role in determining what kind of fish is used in a recipe. For example, a firm-fleshed species, such as cod or haddock, is best for stir-frying because it holds its shape better without becoming mushy. The firmer varieties are also a good bet in dishes like chowders and stews. Flavor, however, is also important. You don't want to mask the delicate taste of something like sole with sauces and seasonings that are too robust.

Since most of the fillets used in these recipes are extremely lean, fat content is not as much a concern, but keep in mind that leaner fish does require basting with some kind of fat when you broil or barbecue it.

Cod has been called "the king of the sea" and remains the most important groundfish species in Atlantic Canada. Cod is a lean, white-fleshed fish which flakes readily when cooked and has a mild flavor. Its relatively firm flesh is moist and pleasant when cooked.

Haddock is a close relative of cod, similar in texture but slightly softer and more refined in flavor. It is lean with white, firm, large-flaked flesh.

Boston bluefish (pollock) is a lean fish with somewhat darker flesh than cod. Boston bluefish can be used in place of cod, haddock or any firm-fleshed fillets in a recipe. It flakes very easily when cooked and has a relatively mild flavor.

Ocean perch (redfish) is traditionally sold with its bright red skin still on. It has lean, medium-firm, snowy-white, moist flesh when cooked, and a relatively mild, somewhat sweet flavor.

Sole is the most important commercial groundfish catch in Atlantic Canada next to cod. It can be any of a variety of flatfishes generally marketed as sole. It is lean with finely grained, soft, white flesh with a delicate, sweet flavor. Since sole fillets are very thin, take care not to overcook them.

If you would like more information about fish fillets and cooking with fish, call the Canadian Seafood Information Centre at 1-800-263-7405.

EASY OPENERS

Don't forget the good fresh taste of fish when you want a first course to pique everyone's appetite. These fast and snappy ideas are not only perfect starters when entertaining but make ideal luncheons accompanied by a dry white wine and crusty bread, followed by a fresh fruit dessert.

The sole is the pivotal species around which European chefs created their masterpieces.
The Encyclopedia of Fish Cookery,
A.J. McClane, Holt, Rinehart & Winston
of Canada, 1987.

SOLE WAVES

These tasty little strips of broiled fish make excellent appetizers served with Raita Sauce. If you use wooden skewers, remember to soak them in water for 20 minutes before threading to avoid charring. For our cover photograph, lime zest was sprinkled over the fish.

1	pkg (280 g) sole fillets, thawed	1
¼ cup	vegetable oil	50 mL
2 tbsp	lime juice	25 mL
1	clove garlic, minced	1

½ tsp	each ground coriander and cumin	2 mL
	Lime slices	
	Raita Sauce	
	(page 81)	

Pat fillets dry with paper towels; place in shallow glass or porcelain baking dish. Stir together oil, lime juice, garlic, coriander and cumin; pour over fish. Cover and refrigerate for at least 30 minutes or up to 2 hours.

Reserving marinade, remove fish and cut fillets lengthwise (with grain) into 1-inch (2.5 cm) strips. Thread each strip at 2-inch (5 cm) intervals onto 6 thin skewers about 9 inches (23 cm) long, adding second strip or short end piece if there's room. Fold very thin strips lengthwise before threading. Place skewers on narrow edges on oiled broiler rack; drizzle with half of the reserved marinade. Broil 4 inches (10 cm) from heat for about 3 minutes per side or until fish flakes with fork, turning once and drizzling with remaining marinade.

Serve hot garnished with lime slices and accompanied by Raita Sauce.

Makes about 5 skewers.

SOLE ST. JACQUES TARTS

A popular appetizer gets updated with a tender pastry crust. Serve as an opener for a dinner party or as the main course for an elegant luncheon.

1 cup	dry white wine	250 mL	2	egg yolks	2
2 tbsp	chopped green onion	25 mL	½ cup	whipping cream	125 mL
¼ tsp	salt	1 mL		Salt and pepper	
Pinch	each black pepper and crushed dried thyme	Pinch	1	pkg (14 oz/397 g) frozen puff pastry, thawed*	1
1	small bay leaf	1			
1 lb	sole fillets, thawed	500 g	1 cup	fine fresh bread crumbs	250 mL
½ lb	mushrooms, sliced	250 g			
1 cup	water	250 mL	¾ cup	shredded Swiss cheese	175 mL
3 tbsp	butter	50 mL			
¼ cup	all-purpose flour	50 mL	4 tsp	butter	20 mL
¾ cup	milk	175 mL		Lemon slices, halved	
Pinch	each cayenne pepper and nutmeg	Pinch		Parsley sprigs	

In shallow medium saucepan, combine wine, onion, salt, black pepper, thyme and bay leaf; simmer for 5 minutes.

Add fish, mushrooms and water. Return to simmer, cover and cook for 5 minutes. Pour into sieve placed over large bowl. Drain well and discard bay leaf. Place in bowl and break fish into large pieces with fork; set aside. Return strained liquid to pan; boil until reduced by half. Measure out 1 cup (250 mL) and keep hot. (Remaining liquid can be frozen for fish stock if desired.)

In medium saucepan, melt butter over medium heat; stir in flour and cook, stirring, for 2 minutes. Remove from heat; whisk in hot poaching liquid, then milk. Season with cayenne and nutmeg. Bring to boil and boil for 1 minute.

In bowl, whisk together egg yolks and cream; gradually beat in hot sauce. Return to pan and cook for 1 minute. Season with salt and pepper to taste. Blend two-thirds of the sauce into fish and mushroom mixture; set aside. Set remaining sauce aside. (Recipe can be prepared ahead to this point, cooled, covered and refrigerated up to 6 hours.)

Divide puff pastry evenly into 8 pieces. On lightly floured surface, roll out pastry to fit 8 large scallop shells or 5-inch (12 cm) shallow tart tins. Ease pastry into shells without stretching it; prick all over with fork. Place on baking sheet and bake in 425°F (220°C) oven for 9 to 10 minutes or until golden but not browned. (Shells can be baked ahead and set aside at room temperature for up to 6 hours.)

Just before serving, gently heat fish mixture and sauce separately. Sprinkle each baked pastry shell with 2 tbsp (25 mL) bread crumbs and evenly spoon fish mixture on top. Pour remaining sauce evenly over fish mixture; sprinkle each with cheese and dot with butter. Broil 5 inches (12 cm) from heat until cheese is melted and bubbly, 1 to 1½ minutes. Garnish with lemon slices and parsley.

*If desired, use your own pie pastry for the shells. You will need the same amount as for 9-inch (23 cm) double crust pie. Prick all over and bake as above for 10 to 12 minutes or until golden.

Makes 8 servings.

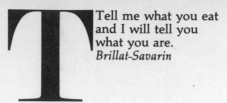

T

Tell me what you eat
and I will tell you
what you are.
Brillat-Savarin

SOLE SEVICHE

Since the acid in citrus juice has the same effect on the protein in fish as heat does, the sole actually "cooks" in lemon and lime juices for this light and refreshing first course. (Photograph opposite page.)

1 lb	sole fillets, thawed	500 g	2 tbsp	chopped fresh coriander	25 mL
½ cup	each lemon and lime juice	125 mL	1	clove garlic, minced	1
¼ cup	finely diced Spanish onion	50 mL	1	tomato, peeled, seeded and diced	1
1 tsp	granulated sugar	5 mL		White pepper	
¼ cup	olive oil	50 mL		Lettuce leaves	
3 tbsp	lime juice	50 mL		Avocado strips	
2 tbsp	diced hot chilies*	25 mL		(optional)	

Cut sole into 1-inch (2.5 cm) pieces; place in glass bowl or dish. Pour in lemon juice and ½ cup (125 mL) lime juice; sprinkle with onion and sugar. Gently stir to mix; cover and refrigerate, stirring occasionally for 3 to 4 hours or until fish is opaque throughout.

Drain well. Stir in oil, 3 tbsp (50 mL) lime juice, chilies, coriander, garlic, tomato, and pepper to taste. Mound on lettuce-lined scallop shells or small plates; garnish with avocado strips if desired.

*If fresh are unavailable, use rinsed canned chilies.

Makes 6 servings.

Sole Seviche
(page 16)

Fish Hot Pot
(page 23)

These shall ye eat of all that are in the waters: whatsoever hath fins and scales in the waters, in the seas, and in the rivers, them shall ye eat.
Leviticus 11:9

FISH-STUFFED SEASHELLS IN TOMATO-TARRAGON CREAM

These attractive stuffed shells, which can be prepared ahead, make a good first course or an easy main course for a casual party.

1	pkg (280 g) fish fillets, frozen	1	¼ tsp	pepper	1 mL
			Pinch	hot pepper flakes	Pinch
½ lb	cream cheese (at room temperature)	250 g	24	large pasta shells (6 oz/175 g)	24
¾ cup	freshly grated Parmesan cheese	175 mL	2 cups	Cream Sauce (page 89)	500 mL
2	cloves garlic, minced	2	2	tomatoes, peeled, seeded and chopped	2
4 tsp	chopped fresh tarragon (or 1 tsp/ 5 mL dried)	20 mL			

Poach fish for about 5 to 7 minutes or until fish flakes with fork (see page 10 for poaching techniques). Let cool and flake; set aside.

In medium bowl, blend together cream cheese, ½ cup (125 mL) Parmesan cheese, garlic, half of the tarragon, pepper and hot pepper flakes; gradually mix in fish. Mixture will be quite stiff. Set aside.

In large pot of boiling salted water, cook pasta until al dente (tender but firm) at centre. Drain well and set aside on tea towel-lined tray in single layer.

Meanwhile, prepare Cream Sauce, doubling recipe on page 89. Season with remaining tarragon. Pour into 13- × 9-inch (3.5 L) baking dish or individual baking dishes; set aside.

Stuff shells with fish mixture; arrange on sauce. (Recipe can be prepared ahead to this point, cooled, covered and refrigerated for up to 24 hours. Remove from refrigerator 30 minutes before proceeding.) Bake, covered, in 400°F (200°C) oven for about 20 minutes or until sauce is bubbly. Sprinkle with tomatoes and remaining Parmesan cheese and serve immediately.

Makes 8 first-course or 4 main-course servings.

For centuries people have believed that fish should be eaten (1) because it is a brain food and (2) because it is easily digested and (3) because it is bloodless and therefore suitable for religious fasts.
The Art of Eating, M.F.K. Fisher, Macmillan Publishing Co., 1954.

COD WITH BLACK BEANS

This easy skillet dish has an interesting, appealing flavor. Serve as an appetizer before a stir-fry supper or as cocktail fare on small plates with forks. You don't really need a garnish, but for a dramatic effect, Chinese long beans and mandarin orange slices look attractive.

1	pkg (280 g) cod fillets, thawed	1	1 tbsp	grated lemon rind	15 mL
¼ cup	cornstarch	50 mL	2 tsp	minced fresh gingerroot	10 mL
¼ cup	lemon juice	50 mL	2 tsp	minced garlic	10 mL
2 tbsp	orange marmalade	25 mL	¼ tsp	pepper	1 mL
2 tbsp	fermented or salted black beans, rinsed*	25 mL	3 tbsp	vegetable oil	50 mL

Pat fish dry with paper towels; cut into 2-inch (5 cm) pieces. Dredge in cornstarch, coating well. Let stand for 30 minutes. (Coated fish can be refrigerated for up to 8 hours.)

In small bowl, stir together lemon juice, orange marmalade, black beans, lemon rind, gingerroot, garlic and pepper; set aside.

In medium skillet, heat oil over medium heat; cook fish, without crowding and in batches if necessary, for 2½ to 3 minutes per side or until golden. Remove to warm platter; cover with foil to keep warm. Add black bean mixture to skillet; cook over medium-high heat for about 30 seconds or until bubbly. Remove from heat and return fish to skillet to lightly coat with sauce.

*Available in oriental grocery stores. Rinse in a sieve under cold water.

Makes 3 or 4 first-course or 8 cocktail servings.

I

I have developed a real respect for frozen fish.
The Art of Eating, M.F.K. Fisher, Macmillan Publishing Co., 1954.

SOLE AND SHRIMP MOUSSE

I enjoyed a crab version of this refreshing mousse as an appetizer at Hotel Paulin in Caraquet, New Brunswick. When I asked owner and chef Gerard Paulin for the recipe, I discovered that his secret ingredient was canned soup. Although canned soups are not usually in my repertoire of ingredients, I felt everyone would very much enjoy this mousse.

Accompany with melba toast or pita triangles brushed with oil, sprinkled liberally with pepper and then broiled.

1	pkg (280 g) sole, frozen	1	¼ lb	cooked shrimp, chopped	125 g
2	envelopes unflavored gelatin	2	½ cup	finely diced celery	125 mL
1	can (10 oz/284 mL) tomato soup (undiluted)	1	½ cup	finely chopped onion	125 mL
			2 tbsp	lemon juice	25 mL
½ lb	cream cheese	250 g	½ tsp	each grated lemon rind and white pepper	2 mL
1 cup	mayonnaise	250 mL		Hot pepper sauce	
				Lettuce leaves	

Poach fish for about 7 minutes or until fish flakes with fork. (See page 10 for poaching technique.) Drain well and chop; set aside.

Sprinkle gelatin over ½ cup (125 mL) cold water; let stand for 5 minutes.

In saucepan, stir together soup and softened gelatin over low heat until gelatin has melted. Remove from heat. Cut cream cheese into small cubes and add to soup; beat with mixer until smooth. Stir in mayonnaise, sole, shrimp, celery, onion, lemon juice, lemon rind, white pepper and 3 or 4 dashes hot pepper sauce.

Transfer to oiled 6-cup (1.5 L) mould or twelve ½-cup (125 mL) moulds; cover and refrigerate for 3 to 4 hours or until firm. Unmould onto lettuce-lined plate or individual salad plates.

Makes 12 appetizers or 6 salad servings.

Seafood products are low in calories. One hundred grams (3½ oz) of low-fat fish such as cod, haddock or sole contains about 80 calories.

SOLE AND SALMON SKEWERS
WITH BASIL-ORANGE SAUCE

Elegant and delicious, these pretty fish skewers make good company fare, either as an appetizer or light main course following a hearty first course.

¼ cup	olive oil	50 mL
1 tbsp	lemon juice	15 mL
Pinch	each salt and pepper	Pinch
1	pkg (280 g) sole fillets, thawed	1
½ lb	salmon fillets or steaks	250 g
½ lb	spinach fettuccine Basil sprigs and orange slices	250 g

Basil-Orange Sauce:

1 tbsp	orange juice	15 mL
1 tbsp	olive oil	15 mL
1 tsp	lemon juice	5 mL
1 tsp	finely grated orange rind	5 mL
¼ cup	cold butter, in bits Salt and pepper	50 mL
½ cup	loosely packed fresh basil leaves, minced	125 mL

In bowl, stir together oil, lemon juice, and salt and pepper to taste. Remove 2 tbsp (25 mL) and set aside. Cut fish into ¾-inch (2 cm) cubes, removing any bones if using salmon steaks. Add to marinade in bowl and toss to coat well. Cover and refrigerate for 30 minutes.

Basil-Orange Sauce: Just before cooking fish, stir together orange juice, oil and lemon juice in small saucepan. Bring to boil over medium-high heat; stir in orange rind. Reduce heat to low and whisk in butter, a few pieces at a time, until sauce is smooth and creamy. Season with salt and pepper to taste. Whisk minced basil into sauce. Keep warm, but do not place over high heat.

Remove fish from marinade and alternately thread sole and salmon onto 8 short skewers. (Skewers can be prepared and refrigerated up to 15 minutes ahead of time.) Prepare a steamer by placing a rack on preserving jar rings or custard cups in roasting pan. Pour in sufficient water to come about ¾-inch (2 cm) below rack; bring to boil.

Meanwhile, in large pot of boiling salted water, cook pasta until al dente (tender but firm). Drain well and return to pan along with 2 tbsp (25 mL) reserved marinade. Toss to coat and keep warm in low oven if necessary.

Place skewers on rack over boiling water; reduce heat to low, cover and steam for 1½ to 2 minutes or until fish is nearly opaque. Uncover steamer while arranging food on plates.

Divide pasta among 8 warm salad plates if using as first course or 4 warm dinner plates if using as main course. Place 1 or 2 skewers on top of each. Drizzle with warm sauce and garnish each plate with basil sprigs and orange slices.

Makes 8 appetizer or 4 main-course servings.

LADLE IT OUT

Whether it's the comforting familiar flavors of steaming Traditional Seafood Chowder (page 27) or the new zest of low-cal Fish Hot Pot (page 23), these soups, stews and chowders are quick and easy with frozen fish fillets.

Solidly frozen fish fillets can be cut into smaller pieces by pressing straight down on the fillet with a heavy chef's knife and rocking the knife back and forth.

Only the pure of heart can
make a good soup.
Ludwig van Beethoven

Soup and fish explain half the
emotions of human life.
Sydney Smith

TOMATO FISH SOUP

For casual Friday night entertaining, serve this hearty main-course soup along with a green salad and crusty French bread. Because most of it can be prepared ahead, it takes only a few minutes to finish.

½ cup	diced rinsed salt pork or side bacon (about 3 oz/90 g)	125 mL
1	large onion, chopped	1
1 cup	diced celery with leaves	250 mL
1 cup	diced peeled potato	250 mL
1 cup	diced carrots	250 mL
1	large clove garlic, minced	1
1	can (28 oz/796 mL) tomatoes (undrained), chopped	1
½ cup	chopped fresh parsley	125 mL
½ cup	dry white wine	125 mL
1 tsp	finely chopped fresh thyme (or ¼ tsp/ 1 mL dried)	5 mL
¼ tsp	pepper	1 mL
	Salt	
1 lb	fish fillets, thawed	500 g

In large saucepan, cook salt pork over medium heat, stirring occasionally, until crisp and browned. Add onion, celery, potato, carrots and garlic; cook, stirring occasionally, for 5 minutes. Stir in tomatoes, parsley, wine, thyme, pepper, and salt to taste; bring to boil. Reduce heat to low; cover and simmer for 30 minutes. (Recipe can be prepared ahead to this point, cooled, covered and refrigerated overnight. Simmer for 10 minutes or until hot before proceeding.)

Just before serving, cut fish into 1-inch (2.5 cm) pieces and add to tomato mixture; cover and cook for about 5 minutes or until fish flakes easily with fork.

Serve in warm soup bowls.

Makes 4 to 6 servings.

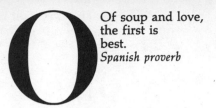

Of soup and love,
the first is
best.
Spanish proverb

FISH HOT POT

This colorful soup with its Oriental flavors is nourishing but low in calories. Pass extra hot chili oil or hot pepper sauce at the table for those who want a more fiery version. If you can find Oriental mushrooms, they make a great substitution for the domestic. (Photograph opposite page 17.)

1	pkg (1.75 oz/50 g) bean thread noodles	1		4	green onions, cut in 1-inch (2.5 cm) pieces	4
2½ cups	chicken broth	625 mL		1 cup	sliced mushrooms (¼ lb/125 g)	250 mL
1	bottle (237 mL) clam juice	1		1 cup	packed shredded bok choy (¼ lb/125 g)	250 mL
2 tbsp	soy sauce	25 mL				
2 tbsp	dry sherry	25 mL		1	pkg (280 g) fish fillets, thawed	1
1 tsp	granulated sugar	5 mL		Dash	hot chili oil or hot pepper sauce	Dash
2	cloves garlic, minced	2				
1	carrot, thinly sliced on diagonal	1				
1	stalk celery, thinly sliced on diagonal	1				

In bowl, cover noodles with warm water; soak for 30 minutes. Drain well and cut into approximately 1½-inch (3 cm) lengths. Set aside.

Meanwhile, in large saucepan, combine chicken broth, clam juice, soy sauce, sherry and sugar. Bring to simmer, stirring to dissolve sugar. Add garlic, carrot, celery and green onions; simmer for 3 minutes. Add mushrooms and bok choy; simmer for 1 minute. Cut fish into 1-inch (2.5 cm) pieces and add to saucepan; simmer for about 2 minutes or until fish flakes easily with fork. Stir in soaked noodles and generous dash of hot chili oil or hot pepper sauce. Serve immediately in heated soup bowls.

Makes 4 to 6 servings.

Since my first bite of fish au vin blanc on the Île de France ... I have been persuaded that it is conceivably the greatest fish preparation in the world. . . .
Cooking with Craig Claiborne and Pierre Franey, Craig Claiborne and Pierre Franey, Fawcett Columbine, 1983.

COD IN WINE SAUCE

This creamy fish stew can be made in less than 30 minutes and makes a wonderful company meal with whole wheat rolls and a green salad.

2 cups	(approx) milk	500 mL
2 lb	cod fillets, frozen	1kg
4 tsp	lemon juice	20 mL
2 tbsp	butter	25 mL
6	green onions, chopped	6
5	stalks celery, chopped	5
1	large sweet green pepper, coarsely chopped	1
½ lb	whole button mushrooms	250 g

Sauce:

½ cup	butter	125 mL
6 tbsp	all-purpose flour	90 mL
¾ cup	dry white wine	175 mL
½ tsp	salt	2 mL
½ tsp	dry mustard	2 mL
½ tsp	dried thyme	2 mL
Pinch	cayenne pepper	Pinch
	Black pepper	
½ cup	whipping cream	125 mL
	Chopped fresh parsley	

In large skillet, pour enough milk over cod to cover, using more milk if necessary; bring to boil. Cover and reduce heat; poach fish for 7 to 10 minutes or until it flakes easily with fork. Do not overcook.

With slotted spoon, remove fillets and chop coarsely. Sprinkle with lemon juice and keep warm. Reserve 2 cups (500 mL) poaching milk for sauce.

In same skillet, melt butter over medium heat; cook onions, celery, green pepper and mushrooms for 3 to 5 minutes or until tender-crisp. Set aside.

Sauce: In large saucepan, melt butter over medium heat; stir in flour and cook, stirring, without browning, for 3 minutes. Remove from heat and gradually whisk in reserved warm milk and wine. Add salt, mustard, thyme, cayenne, and black pepper to taste; cook over medium-low heat for 5 to 10 minutes or until desired thickness is reached. Reduce heat to low and gradually whisk in cream. Heat through but do not boil.

Stir in cod and cooked vegetables; heat through but do not boil. Taste and adjust seasoning. Serve garnished with parsley.

Makes 8 servings.

To make a good soup, the pot must only simmer or 'smile.'
French proverb

I live on good soup, not on fine words.
Molière

FISH SOUP JARDINIÈRE

This main-course soup, loaded with garden vegetables, is light and fresh-tasting but just as satisfying as heavier soups or stews. In the photograph opposite page 32, small-leafed (bush) basil was used to garnish the dish but you can use parsley.

2 tbsp	vegetable oil	25 mL	
2 cups	sliced mushrooms (½ lb/250 g)	500 mL	
1 cup	thinly sliced leeks	250 mL	
1	clove garlic, minced	1	
3 cups	water	750 mL	
2 cups	torn Boston or leaf lettuce	500 mL	
3	small carrots, quartered	3	
2	stalks celery, cut in ½-inch (1 cm) diagonal slices	2	
2	large sprigs thyme (or ¾ tsp/4 mL dried)	2	
½ tsp	salt	2 mL	
¼ tsp	pepper	1 mL	
1	bay leaf	1	
6	small red potatoes, quartered (about ¾ lb/375 g)	6	
2	small zucchini, cut in ½-inch (1 cm) slices	2	
1 lb	fish fillets (cod, sole or haddock), thawed and cut in 1-inch (2.5 cm) pieces	500 g	
	Chopped fresh parsley		

In large saucepan, heat oil over medium heat; cook mushrooms, leeks and garlic for 2 minutes without browning. Stir in water, lettuce, carrots, celery, thyme, salt, pepper and bay leaf. Bring to a boil; cover, reduce heat and simmer for 10 minutes.

Add potatoes and zucchini; simmer for 8 to 10 minutes longer or just until vegetables become tender-crisp.

Add fish and simmer for 5 minutes or until fish is opaque and flakes easily with fork. Discard bay leaf. Taste and adjust seasoning. Ladle into large hot soup bowls; garnish with parsley.

Makes 4 to 6 servings.

Stepping to the kitchen door, I uttered the word 'cod' with great emphasis, and resumed my seat. In a few moments the savory steam came forth again, but with a different flavor, and in good time a fine cod-chowder was placed before us.
Herman Melville, Moby Dick

SUMMER HARVEST FISH CHOWDER WITH PESTO TOASTS

This light, colorful chowder celebrates the combination of fish and summer vegetables with a burst of extra flavor from the pesto-topped toasts. (Photograph opposite page 32).

	French baguette			Salt and pepper	
	Pesto Sauce (page 90)		1 lb	cod or haddock fillets,	500 g
¼ cup	butter	50 mL		frozen or thawed, cut	
2	carrots, thinly sliced	2		in 1-inch (2.5 cm)	
1	onion, chopped	1		pieces	
2	cloves garlic, minced	2	1 cup	fresh or frozen corn	250 mL
1	small zucchini, thinly	1		kernels	
	sliced		1	large tomato, peeled,	1
1	bottle (237 mL) clam	1		seeded and coarsely	
	juice			chopped	
1 cup	water or chicken stock	250 mL	2 cups	milk	500 mL
½ tsp	chopped fresh basil	2 mL			
	(or pinch dried)				

Slice eight ½-inch (1 cm) thick slices from baguette. Bake in single layer on baking sheet in 400°F (200°C) oven for 8 to 10 minutes or until browned. Spread about 1½ tsp (7 mL) Pesto Sauce on one side of each slice and set aside.

In large saucepan, melt butter over medium heat; cook carrots, onion and garlic, stirring occasionally, for 5 minutes. Add zucchini and cook for 3 minutes.

Stir in clam juice, water, basil, and salt and pepper to taste; simmer for 10 minutes. Add fish if frozen and simmer for 3 minutes. If thawed, add along with corn and tomato; simmer for 3 minutes or until fish flakes easily with fork. Stir in milk and heat through. Taste and adjust seasoning. Ladle into warm soup bowls and top each with pesto crouton.

Makes 4 main-course servings or 8 first-course servings.

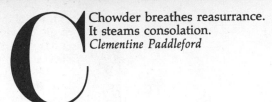

*Chowder breathes reasurrance.
It steams consolation.*
Clementine Paddleford

TRADITIONAL
SEAFOOD CHOWDER

An old-fashioned, hearty chowder is comforting
and delicious when winter winds blow. You can cut
completely frozen fillets if you use a heavy, sharp
knife.

1 lb	cod or haddock fillets, frozen or thawed	500 g	½ cup	sliced mushrooms	125 mL
¼ tsp	salt	1 mL	2 tbsp	all-purpose flour	25 mL
1	bay leaf	1	1¼ cups	milk	300 mL
2 tbsp	butter	25 mL	¾ cup	small cooked shrimp (about 4 oz/125 g)	175 mL
¼ lb	salt pork	125 g		Salt and pepper	
3	potatoes, cut in ½-inch (1 cm) cubes	3		Lemon juice	
1	onion, chopped	1	2 tbsp	chopped fresh parsley	25 mL
				Croutons	

Cut fish into 1-inch (2.5 cm) cubes. In
saucepan, bring 2¼ cups (550 mL) water
to boil. Add fish, salt and bay leaf;
reduce heat to low and simmer, covered,
for 5 minutes if fish is thawed, 7 to 10
minutes if frozen, or until fish flakes
with fork. Drain and reserve liquid;
discard bay leaf.

Meanwhile, rinse salt pork well and
dry; dice finely. In large saucepan, melt
butter over medium heat; cook salt pork
until crisp and brown. Remove with
slotted spoon and set aside. Pour off all
but 2 tbsp (25 mL) fat. Add potatoes,
onion and mushrooms to saucepan;
cook over medium heat for 5 minutes.
Stir in flour and cook for 1 minute,
stirring. Gradually stir in reserved cooking liquid and milk; bring to boil.
Reduce heat, cover and simmer for 5 to
10 minutes or until potatoes are tender.

Add cooked fish along with shrimp to
pan; heat through. Season to taste with
salt, pepper and lemon juice; stir in
parsley. Serve in heated soup bowls
sprinkled with salt pork and croutons.

Makes 4 generous servings.

I

I'm fond of anything that comes out of the sea — and that includes sailors.
Janet Flanner

FISHERMAN'S STEW

This bright fresh stew, or cioppino, is just right for inexpensive, casual entertaining. (It can easily be doubled for a larger crowd.) Begin the meal with marinated olives, accompany the stew with crusty Italian bread and beer, and follow it with a salad of leaf lettuce, red onion and goat cheese.

2 tbsp	olive oil	25 mL	¼ tsp	each black pepper and hot pepper flakes	1 mL
1	large onion, chopped	1			
4	cloves garlic, minced	4	2	bay leaves	2
1	sweet pepper (green, yellow or red), diced	1	2	pkg (each 280 g) haddock or cod fillets, thawed	2
1	can (28 oz/796 mL) tomatoes (undrained)	1	8	mussels, scrubbed and beards removed	8
1	bottle (237 mL) clam juice	1	¼ cup	chopped fresh parsley	50 mL
1½ tsp	finely chopped fresh thyme (or ½ tsp dried crushed)	7 mL	2 tbsp	chopped green onion Garlic Mayonnaise or Roasted Garlic Mayonnaise (page 83)	25 mL
½ tsp	fennel seed	2 mL			

In large heavy saucepan, heat oil over medium heat; cook onion, garlic and sweet pepper until softened, about 5 minutes. Add tomatoes, crushing with potato masher or breaking up with spoon. Stir in clam juice, thyme, fennel seed, black pepper, hot pepper flakes and bay leaves. Bring to boil, reduce heat and simmer, uncovered and stirring occasionally, for 12 to 15 minutes or until slightly thickened. (Stew can be made ahead to this point, cooled, covered and refrigerated for up to 2 days. Bring to simmer before continuing.)

Cut fish into 2-inch (5 cm) pieces and add to tomato mixture; cover and cook over medium-low heat for 3 minutes. Add mussels, pushing them down into tomato mixture. Do not stir, but baste fish with liquid. Cover and simmer for another 3 minutes or until fish flakes with fork and mussels open. Discard any mussels that do not open. Discard bay leaves. Sprinkle with parsley and green onion. Ladle into heated soup bowls. Spoon some Garlic Mayonnaise onto centre of each serving.

Makes 4 to 6 servings.

WHAT'S FOR SUPPER?

Time is short and you're tired, but when the inevitable question is asked — "What's for supper?" — you want to provide a dinner that's nutritious and interesting. Here are main-course dishes that allow you to answer the question in dozens of ways and satisfy family members and casual company alike.

Any fish eaten two or three times a week is believed to lower blood pressure and blood fat and thereby may reduce the risk of heart disease.

BAKED FISH RATATOUILLE

Fresh garden vegetables and lean fish combine to make an easy one-dish meal that's low in calories.

1	small eggplant	1	½ tsp	each finely chopped fresh thyme and basil (or pinch dried)	2 mL
	Salt				
2 tbsp	vegetable oil	25 mL			
1	onion, finely chopped	1	2 tbsp	chopped fresh parsley	25 mL
1	small clove garlic, minced	1		Pepper	
2	small zucchini, sliced	2	1 tsp	drained capers	5 mL
1	small sweet green pepper, cut in chunks	1	1 lb	cod fillets, thawed	500 g
2	large tomatoes, peeled, seeded and coarsely chopped	2			

Peel and dice eggplant; place in colander and sprinkle with salt. Let stand for 20 minutes. Rinse with cold water and pat dry.

In skillet, heat oil over medium heat; cook onion and garlic for 3 minutes. Add eggplant, zucchini and green pepper; cook for 5 minutes. Stir in tomatoes, thyme and basil; bring to boil. Cover and reduce heat; simmer for 7 to 10 minutes or until zucchini is tender-crisp. Stir in parsley, and salt and pepper to taste. (Recipe can be prepared ahead to this point, cooled, covered and refrigerated for several days or frozen for up to 3 months. Bring to room temperature before proceeding.) Stir in capers.

Pat fish dry with paper towel and arrange fillets in single layer in greased shallow baking dish. Spoon eggplant mixture over top and bake, covered, in 350°F (180°C) oven for 12 to 15 minutes or until fish flakes easily with fork.

Makes 4 servings.

Like most Southerners, I adore catfish. I'm not certain that my mother ever prepared catfish at home, however. She was too aristocratic for that.
Cooking with Craig Claiborne and Pierre Franey, Craig Claiborne and Pierre Franey, Fawcett Columbine, 1983.

CAJUN FRIES

These spicy deep-fried fish strips will be very popular with the supper crowd. Serve them with a sauce, if you like, or a generous sprinkle of lemon juice.

1	egg	1		¼ cup	all-purpose flour	50 mL
¼ cup	milk	50 mL		1 tsp	cayenne pepper	5 mL
2 tsp	olive oil	10 mL		½ tsp	black pepper	2 mL
2 tsp	garlic powder	10 mL		¼ tsp	salt	1 mL
1 tsp	dried lemon peel	5 mL		1 cup	fine cracker crumbs (about 32)	250 mL
½ tsp	each dried oregano and thyme	2 mL			Vegetable oil for deep-frying	
1 lb	haddock, cod, or ocean perch fillets, thawed	500 g				

In shallow bowl, beat together egg, milk, oil, garlic powder, dried peel, oregano and thyme. Set aside.

Remove skin from perch if using. Cut fillets in half crosswise, then cut halves lengthwise into 1½-inch (4 cm) strips. Pat dry with paper towels. Set aside.

In shallow bowl, stir together flour, cayenne, black pepper and salt. Spread cracker crumbs on waxed paper. Coat each fish strip well in flour mixture, then dip into egg mixture; roll in crumbs to coat well.

Pour enough oil into deep-fryer or heavy saucepan to come about 3½ inches (9 cm) up sides of pan; heat until deep-frying thermometer registers 375°F (190°C). Cook fish strips in batches and without crowding, turning with spoon, for 2 to 2½ minutes or until golden and fish flakes easily with fork. Remove strips when cooked to drain on wire rack set over plate, or on crumpled paper towels.

Makes about 4 servings.

The warm waters of the northerly flowing Gulf Stream mingling with the frigid Labrador current create conditions particularly conducive to sustaining large populations of cod, haddock and other groundfish species.

PENNE WITH SPICY TOMATO AND FISH SAUCE

Made with ingredients you probably have on hand, this is a fast, simple and thrifty main dish. Add a green salad and crusty bread for a supper that's sure to become a family favorite. Just halve the recipe for two. If you prefer, use corkscrew pasta instead of straight tubular macaroni. (Photograph opposite page 33.)

¼ cup	olive oil	50 mL
3	cloves garlic, minced	3
¼ tsp	(approx) hot pepper flakes	1 mL
1 tsp	anchovy paste	5 mL
1	can (19 oz/540 mL) tomatoes (undrained)	1
½ tsp	salt	2 mL
¼ tsp	pepper	1 mL
1 lb	fish fillets, frozen or thawed, cut in 1-inch (2.5 cm) pieces	500 g
⅓ cup	chopped fresh parsley	75 mL
¾ lb	penne (tubular macaroni)	375 g

In large skillet, heat oil over medium-low heat, cook garlic until softened, but not browned, about 5 minutes; remove pan from heat. Stir in hot pepper flakes, adding more to taste if desired; stir in anchovy paste, then tomatoes. Return to medium heat; stir in salt and pepper. Bring to simmer, breaking up tomatoes with wooden spoon. Cook, uncovered and stirring often, for about 15 minutes or until thickened.

Stir in fish and half of the parsley. Simmer for 6 minutes if fish is frozen, 3 minutes if thawed or until fish flakes easily with fork.

Meanwhile, in large pot of boiling salted water, cook penne until al dente (tender but firm). Drain well and toss with tomato-fish sauce in large warm serving bowl. Sprinkle with remaining parsley.

Makes 4 servings.

Summer Harvest
Fish Chowder with
Pesto Toasts
(page 26)

Fish Soup Jardinière
(page 25)

Baked Stuffed Cod
(page 33)

Penne with
Spicy Tomato
and Fish
Sauce
(page 32)

Sole in
Lettuce Packages
(page 69)

According to the *Nova Scotia Department of Fisheries*, seafood is one of the healthiest foods you can eat, providing all the essential amino acids and many of the vitamins and minerals your body needs. The minimum of fat it does contain is polyunsaturated.

BAKED STUFFED COD

Elizabeth Baird learned from Sadie Rowe of Heart's Content, Newfoundland, that putting stuffing between two equal-sized fillets is much easier and quicker than stuffing a whole fish. Elizabeth passes along her adaptation here. (Photograph opposite page.)

1 lb	cod fillets, thawed	500 g	½ tsp	salt		2 mL
¼ cup	butter	50 mL	¼ tsp	pepper		1 mL
1	onion, minced	1	1½	coarse slightly stale		375 mL
1	small carrot, diced	1	cups	bread crumbs		
2 tbsp	chopped fresh savory (or 2 tsp/10 mL dried)	25 mL				

Pat fish dry with paper towels; place half of the fillets in greased shallow baking dish. Set remaining fillets aside.

In small skillet, melt butter; pour off half and reserve. Add onion and carrot to skillet; cook over medium heat until softened, about 5 minutes. Stir in savory, salt and pepper; cook for 2 minutes. Remove from heat; stir in bread crumbs.

Equally divide bread crumb mixture and mound on each fillet in dish; top with reserved fillets. Drizzle reserved butter over top and bake, uncovered, in 400°F (200°C) oven for 15 to 20 minutes or until fish flakes with fork.

Makes 4 servings.

F Fish and guests grow stale in three days.
Chinese proverb

ORIENTAL STEAMED COD

Steaming fish right on the same plate with a variety of vegetables results in a very quick and delicious supper. For one hearty serving, cut the amount of fish in half and reduce the vegetables slightly. Serve with hot, fluffy rice.

2 tbsp	soy sauce	25 mL		½ cup	finely shredded cabbage	125 mL
4 tsp	rice wine, dry white wine or chicken stock	20 mL		3	green onions	3
1	thin slice gingerroot, finely slivered	1		1	pkg (280 g) cod fillets, thawed	1
½ tsp	Oriental sesame oil (optional)	2 mL		2	carrots, in thin julienned strips	2
1	clove garlic, minced	1				

In small bowl, stir together soy sauce, rice wine, gingerroot, sesame oil (if using) and garlic.

Spread cabbage evenly in 9- or 10-inch (23 or 25 cm) glass pie plate or deep-rimmed heatproof plate. Chop 1 of the green onions; sprinkle over cabbage. Cut remaining onions into thin julienned pieces and set aside.

Sprinkle cabbage mixture with 4 tsp (20 mL) of the soy mixture. Arrange fish on top, overlapping thin ends of fillets if necessary. Surround fish with julienned green onions and carrots. Pour remaining soy sauce mixture over top.

Fit rack or ring of crumpled foil into large skillet or shallow saucepan large enough to hold plate with a bit of room around plate for steam to circulate. Pour enough water into skillet to come just under rack. Bring to boil; reduce heat to simmer. Place plate on rack and cover skillet. Steam for 4½ to 5 minutes or until fish is opaque in centre and flakes with fork.

Makes 2 servings.

> In cooking, as in all the arts,
> simplicity is the sign
> of perfection.
> *Curnonsky*

FISH FILLETS BAKED WITH PARSLEY CRUMBS

This colorful fish and rice combination makes a good family or company casserole. Serve with a salad of strong greens such as curly endive.

¾ cup	long-grain rice	175 mL
2	pkg (each 280 g) sole fillets, thawed	2
	Salt and pepper	
2 tbsp	dry vermouth	25 mL
¼ cup	coarsely chopped pitted black olives	50 mL
2	tomatoes, peeled and sliced	2
⅓ cup	butter	75 mL
1	onion, minced	1
2	cloves garlic, minced	2
1½ cups	coarse fresh bread crumbs	375 mL
½ cup	chopped fresh parsley	125 mL
	Lemon slices	

In small saucepan, bring rice and 1 cup (250 mL) water to boil; reduce heat, cover and simmer for 5 minutes. (Rice will not be fully cooked.) Spread in greased shallow 8- or 9-inch (2 or 2.5 L) square baking dish. Sprinkle fish with salt and pepper to taste; arrange over rice, overlapping thin ends of fish if necessary. Sprinkle with vermouth; scatter olives over top. Arrange tomato slices in single layer over olives. Sprinkle lightly with salt and pepper to taste. (Recipe can be prepared to this point, covered and refrigerated up to 6 hours.)

In small skillet, melt butter over medium heat; cook onion, garlic and sprinkle of salt and pepper for about 5 minutes or until softened. Remove from heat and let cool slightly. Add bread crumbs and parsley; toss to mix. Sprinkle over tomatoes; bake in 350°F (180°C) oven for about 25 minutes or until fish is opaque and flakes easily with fork and topping is golden brown. Garnish with lemon slices.

Makes 4 servings.

Don't overcook [fish]. Most people do. . . . Nothing is less palatable than overcooked fish, which has become soft and mushy, losing both texture and flavor.
Delights and Prejudices, James Beard, Atheneum, 1964.

TANDOORI FILLETS

Served with parsleyed rice or potatoes and green peas, these simple broiled fillets make an easy and interesting supper.

⅓ cup	plain yogurt (not low-fat)	75 mL	¼ tsp	salt	1 mL
3 tbsp	soft butter	50 mL	Pinch	each black and cayenne peppers	Pinch
½ tsp	each ground coriander, ground cumin and grated fresh gingerroot	2 mL	2	cloves garlic, crushed	2
			1 lb	fish fillets, thawed	500 g

In small bowl, whisk together yogurt and butter; stir in coriander, cumin, gingerroot, salt, pepper, cayenne and garlic.

Pat fish dry with paper towels; arrange in single layer in greased shallow baking dish just big enough to hold fillets snugly. Spread evenly with yogurt mixture; let stand for 30 minutes at room temperature.

Leave in pan and broil about 4 inches (10 cm) from heat, without turning, for 5 to 7 minutes or until fish flakes with fork and is golden brown.

Makes 3 or 4 servings.

GINGER CHILI FISH

A very light, crisp batter and an interesting Chinese sauce combine to make this deep-fried fish a memorable meal. Garnish with green onion curls (see page 50). Serve with steamed rice and stir-fried crisp vegetables.

1 lb	fish fillets, thawed	500 g
¾ cup	water	175 mL
⅔ cup	all-purpose flour	150 mL
⅓ cup	cornstarch	75 mL
1	egg white	1
2 tsp	vegetable oil	10 mL
1 tsp	granulated sugar	5 mL
1 tsp	baking powder	5 mL
½ tsp	salt	2 mL
Pinch	white pepper	Pinch
	Peanut or vegetable oil for deep-frying	

Sauce:

1	can (7½ oz/213 mL) tomato sauce	1
¼ cup	chicken broth	50 mL
2 tbsp	dry sherry or rice wine	25 mL
1 tbsp	each grated fresh gingerroot, soy sauce, water and granulated sugar	15 mL
2 tsp	cornstarch	10 mL
½ tsp	chili oil	2 mL
3	cloves garlic, crushed	3

Sauce: In small saucepan, stir together tomato sauce, chicken broth, sherry, gingerroot, soy sauce, water, sugar, cornstarch, chili oil and garlic. Bring to boil over medium heat and boil, stirring constantly, for 2 minutes; remove from heat. (Sauce can be prepared ahead and reheated just as you finish cooking fish.)

Cut fillets into 1½-inch (4 cm) pieces: pat dry with paper towels. In medium bowl, whisk together water, flour, cornstarch, egg white, oil, sugar, baking powder, salt and white pepper until smooth.

In wok or shallow large saucepan, heat 2 to 3 inches (5 to 8 cm) oil until deep-fryer thermometer registers 375°F (190°C). Dip fish pieces, a few at a time, into batter; let excess drip off. Cook fish, in batches and without crowding, for 1½ to 2 minutes or until golden brown and flakes easily with a fork. Drain on crumpled paper towels. Serve immediately with hot sauce.

Makes 4 servings.

PARMESAN BAKED FILLETS

These quick, easy fillets can be teamed with steamed broccoli and baked potato slices (recipe, next page) for a simple but delicious supper.

½ cup	mayonnaise	125 mL		¼ cup	each dry bread crumbs and freshly grated Parmesan cheese	50 mL
¼ cup	finely chopped fresh parsley	50 mL				
½ tsp	finely chopped fresh thyme (or pinch dried)	2 mL		1	pkg (280 g) fish fillets, thawed	1

In small bowl, stir together mayonnaise, parsley and thyme. On waxed paper, mix together bread crumbs and cheese. Pat fish dry with paper towels; spread mayonnaise mixture on both sides of fillets. Dip in crumb mixture. Arrange on greased baking sheet (or lined with greased foil if you wish). (Recipe can be prepared ahead, covered and refrigerated up to 6 hours.)

Bake in 450°F (230°C) oven for 8 to 10 minutes or until fish flakes with fork.

Makes 2 or 3 servings.

OVEN-BAKED POTATO SLICES

Crisp and delicious, these oven-baked slices rival potato chips because they are cooked with hardly any fat and much less bother than deep-frying.

4	large potatoes	4	1 tsp	paprika	5 mL
2 tbsp	each vegetable oil and butter	25 mL	¼ tsp	each crushed dried thyme and rosemary	1 mL
1	clove garlic, minced	1		Salt	

Peel and slice potatoes no thicker than ¼ inch (5 mm), dropping slices into bowl of cold water as you work.

Line 15- × 10-inch (2 L) jelly-roll pan with foil. Combine oil, butter, garlic, paprika, thyme and rosemary on foil; heat in 450°F (230°C) oven just until butter melts, watching that it doesn't brown. Stir gently to combine seasonings.

Drain potatoes well and pat dry. Place in butter mixture and turn to coat well; spread out as much as possible and bake for 15 minutes. With spatula, turn potatoes and bake for another 10 to 15 minutes or until golden and edges are crisp. Sprinkle with salt to taste and serve immediately.

Makes 4 servings.

VARIATION:

Parmesan Baked Potato Slices

After slices have baked 15 minutes, turn and sprinkle with 1 tbsp (15 mL) lemon juice and 2 tbsp (25 mL) freshly grated Parmesan cheese. Bake for another 10 minutes or until edges are crisp. Omit the salt.

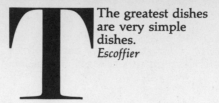

T The greatest dishes
are very simple
dishes.
Escoffier

BAKED FILLETS WITH
VEGETABLE CHEESE CROWN

Fast and easy to make, this colorful main course is
low in calories, but high in flavor.

1	pkg (280 g) fish fillets, thawed	1	¼ cup	each grated carrot and diced seeded tomato	50 mL
	Salt and pepper				
¼ cup	lemon juice	50 mL	¼ cup	minced onion or shallot	50 mL
1 cup	shredded mild Cheddar cheese (about ¼ lb/125 g)	250 mL	2 tbsp	finely chopped fresh parsley	25 mL

Pat fish dry with paper towels; arrange in single layer in greased baking dish. Sprinkle with salt and pepper to taste; drizzle with half of the lemon juice.

In small bowl, stir together cheese, remaining lemon juice, carrot, tomato, onion and parsley. Mound evenly over fillets, spreading almost to edges.

(Recipe can be prepared ahead to this point, covered and refrigerated up to 4 hours.)

Bake, loosely covered, in 400°F (200°C) oven for 12 to 15 minutes or just until fish starts to flake with fork. Uncover and bake for 5 minutes longer or until cheese is melted and bubbly.

Makes 2 or 3 servings.

Fish is 'brain' food.

This bit of folk wisdom may be partially true since recent studies have suggested that the fatty acids in fish may be involved in the development of neural tissue.

TERIYAKI BAKED FILLETS

Serve this easy dish with steamed rice along with stir-fried snow peas and carrots for a quick meal the whole family will love.

3 tbsp	tamari (natural soy sauce) or light soy sauce	50 mL		2 tsp	vegetable oil	10 mL
				1	small clove garlic, minced	1
2 tbsp	dry sherry	25 mL		1 lb	haddock, cod or perch fillets, thawed	500 g
2 tsp	granulated sugar	10 mL				
2 tsp	grated fresh gingerroot	10 mL				

In small bowl, stir together tamari, sherry, sugar, gingerroot, oil and garlic. Pat fish dry with paper towels; arrange in single layer in baking dish just big enough to hold fillets snugly. Pour marinade over top; cover and refrigerate for at least 1 hour or up to 4 hours.

Bake, uncovered, in 450°F (230°C) oven for 8 to 10 minutes or until fish flakes with fork.

Makes 3 to 4 servings.

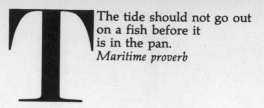

T

The tide should not go out on a fish before it is in the pan.
Maritime proverb

SPICY PAN-FRIED FILLETS

Accompany this simple sautéed fish with Horse-radish Mayonnaise, Mustard Mayonnaise or Thousand Island Sauce (pages 83 and 85).

1 lb	fish fillets, thawed	500 g	2 tbsp	each butter and vegetable oil	25 mL
3 tbsp	each lemon juice and Worcestershire sauce	50 mL		Lemon wedges and parsley sprigs	
½ cup	all-purpose flour	125 mL			
Pinch	each salt and pepper	Pinch			

Pat fillets very dry with paper towels. In shallow dish, stir together lemon juice and Worcestershire sauce. In another dish, stir together flour, salt and pepper.

Dip fish in lemon mixture, then in flour mixture, shaking off any excess.

(Fish can be prepared ahead, covered and refrigerated for up to 6 hours.)

In large skillet, melt butter with oil over medium-high heat; cook fish for 1½ to 2 minutes per side or until golden. Serve immediately garnished with lemon wedges and parsley.

Makes 3 or 4 servings.

C . . . Canadian literature, coast to coast, is literally squirming with fish. Seems they're as important in the minds of the writers as they are in those of government negotiators, a rare overlap.
The CanLit Foodbook, Margaret Atwood, Totem Books, 1987.

BROILED FISH WITH GARLIC-LEMON BUTTER

Zesty butter keeps the fish beautifully moist during broiling. Serve with creamed potatoes and buttered baby beets for a quick and delicious supper.

3 tbsp	butter (at room temperature)	50 mL	Pinch	salt	Pinch
2	cloves garlic, minced	2	1 lb	fish fillets, thawed	500 g
2 tbsp	minced fresh parsley	25 mL	2 tbsp	lemon juice	25 mL
½ tsp	grated lemon rind	2 mL		Lemon wedges and parsley sprigs	

In small bowl, cream butter; blend in garlic, parsley, lemon rind and salt. Pat fish dry with paper towels; arrange in well-greased broiling pan. Sprinkle with lemon juice; spread with butter mixture. (Recipe can be prepared ahead to this point, covered and refrigerated for up to 6 hours.)

Broil about 4 inches (10 cm) from heat for about 7 minutes or until fish flakes with fork. Don't turn. Transfer to heated platter and pour pan juices over fish. Garnish with lemon wedges and parsley.

Makes 3 or 4 servings.

MUSTARD BAKED SOLE

In this simple treatment, the sole stays very moist and flavorful. Accompany with crisp green beans and crunchy slices of potato (see page 39 for Oven-baked Potato Slices) for a fast and easy but elegant supper.

¼ cup	butter	50 mL		1 tbsp	Dijon mustard	15 mL
	Salt and pepper			¼ cup	fine fresh bread crumbs	50 mL
¼ cup	minced onion	50 mL				
1 lb	sole fillets, thawed	500 g		1 tbsp	minced fresh parsley	15 mL
¼ cup	dry white wine or chicken stock	50 mL			Lemon wedges	

Line small baking sheet with foil; spread with 1 tbsp (15 mL) of the butter. Sprinkle sheet lightly with salt and pepper; scatter onion evenly over top. Pat fish dry with paper towels; arrange on top of onion. Sprinkle fish with 2 tbsp (25 mL) of the wine.

In small bowl, blend together remaining wine and mustard; spread over fish. Sprinkle evenly with bread crumbs and dot with remaining butter. Bake in 500°F (260°C) oven for 8 to 10 minutes or until fish flakes with fork and fillets are golden. Sprinkle with parsley and serve immediately garnished with lemon wedges.

Makes 3 or 4 servings.

Almost 7 billion pounds of cod are landed each year by vessels of all nations.
The Encyclopedia of Fish Cookery,
A.J. McClane, Holt, Rinehart, & Winston
of Canada, 1987.

COD CAKES

Accompany with Horseradish Mayonnaise (page 83), Tartar Sauce (page 80) or hot Creole Sauce (page 91) and serve a good mixed vegetable salad with these easy old-fashioned fish cakes. Or, serve cakes in toasted buns for fishburgers.

1 lb	cod fillets	500 g		¼ cup	chopped fresh parsley	50 mL
3 cups	mashed cooked potatoes	750 mL		1 tsp	prepared horseradish	5 mL
2	eggs, beaten	2			Salt and pepper	
¼ cup	chopped onion	50 mL		⅓ cup	all-purpose flour	75 mL
				¼ cup	(approx) vegetable oil	50 mL

Poach cod for about 5 minutes for thawed, 7 to 10 minutes for frozen, or until fish flakes with fork. (See page 10 for poaching technique.) Drain well and flake with fork.

In large bowl, stir together fish, mashed potatoes, eggs, onion, parsley, horseradish, and salt and pepper to taste.

In shallow dish, season flour with salt and pepper to taste. Shape fish mixture into twelve 3½-inch (9 cm) patties and coat lightly with seasoned flour. (If time permits, refrigerate patties for 30 minutes because they will hold together better during cooking.)

In large skillet, heat oil over medium heat; fry patties for 2 to 3 minutes per side or until crisp and golden, adding more oil if necessary. Drain on crumpled paper towels and serve hot.

Makes 4 to 6 servings.

ORANGE POACHED FISH

Serve this quick and easy skillet supper with hot rice
and a spinach salad.

1 cup	orange juice	250 mL	1 lb	ocean perch or cod	500 g
2 tbsp	dry sherry	25 mL		fillets, thawed	
1 tbsp	soy sauce	15 mL		Salt	
¼ tsp	pepper	1 mL	½ cup	fish or chicken stock*	125 mL
3	carrots, thinly sliced	3	2 tsp	cornstarch	10 mL
2	onions, sliced	2		Chopped fresh	
1	sweet red pepper, cut in strips	1		parsley	

In large skillet, stir together orange
juice, sherry, soy sauce and pepper. Add
carrots and onions; bring to boil. Reduce
heat, cover and simmer for 8 minutes or
until vegetables are tender-crisp. Stir in
red pepper; push vegetables to edge of
pan.

Sprinkle fish lightly with salt to taste.
Arrange in centre of skillet; bring to boil.
Reduce heat to medium-low, cover and
simmer for 2 to 3 minutes or until fish
flakes with fork. With slotted spoon,
remove fish and keep warm under tent
of foil.

In cup, stir together stock and cornstarch; stir into skillet and cook over
medium heat, stirring, until thickened.
Cook for 2 more minutes. Return fish to
skillet and heat through. Taste and
adjust seasoning. Sprinkle with parsley
to serve.
*Powdered fish stock is available in
delicatessens.

Makes 4 servings.

Gastronomically, cod belongs to that interesting group of foods distinguished by a more or less neutral flavor that complements . . . a host of other flavors. . . .
Craig Claiborne's Favorites from The New York Times, Craig Claiborne, Times Books, 1976.

LEMON-PARSLEY SHELLS WITH COD NUGGETS

An easy cream sauce, sautéed fish and hot pasta make a quick but satisfying one-dish supper everyone will love. Toss a green salad to go alongside, and accompany with extra grated Parmesan to sprinkle on individual servings.

1 cup	whipping cream	250 mL
¼ cup	butter	50 mL
¼ tsp	salt	1 mL
Pinch	each nutmeg and cayenne pepper	Pinch
¼ cup	freshly grated Parmesan cheese	50 mL
½ cup	chopped fresh parsley	125 mL
¼ cup	snipped chives or green onion tops	50 mL
1 lb	cod fillets, cut in 1½-inch (4 cm) chunks*	500 g
½ lb	medium shell pasta	250 g
1 tsp	grated lemon rind	5 mL

In small heavy saucepan, stir together cream, half of the butter, salt, nutmeg and cayenne; simmer over medium heat for 10 minutes or until slightly thickened. Whisk in cheese, then ⅓ cup (75 mL) of the parsley and the chives; simmer for 5 minutes. Taste and adjust seasoning.

In large skillet, melt remaining butter over medium heat; cook cod chunks for about 3 minutes or until they start to flake with fork. Add to sauce and simmer for 1 minute.

Meanwhile, in large pot of boiling salted water, cook pasta until al dente, (tender but firm), 7 to 10 minutes. Drain well and toss with half of the sauce. Turn out onto platter and top with remaining sauce; sprinkle with lemon rind and remaining parsley.

*If you wish, the fillets can be cut into chunks when partially thawed. Drain the chunks well and press as dry as possible with paper towels.

Makes 4 to 6 servings.

D Depending on whether you find small soft-shelled clams or large hard-shelled ones, steaming will vary from 3 to 10 minutes. You might like to steam the clams in a tightly covered saucepan with a little water and add to the other cooked ingredients. The clams will take longer to open when cooked with the rice.

EASY FAMILY PAELLA

A complete meal in one dish, this quick paella is colorful, inexpensive and nutritious. It's great for casual entertaining too. Chorizo is a spicy Spanish sausage. If unavailable, substitute any hot, spicy sausage. (Photograph opposite page.)

½ lb	hot Italian sausage, chorizo or other spicy sausage	250 g	¼ tsp	each turmeric and pepper	1 mL
2 tbsp	olive oil	25 mL	2¼ cups	hot chicken stock or fish stock*	550 mL
4	green onions, chopped	4	8	small clams, scrubbed	8
1	sweet red or green pepper, cut in strips	1	8	mussels, scrubbed and beards removed	8
2	cloves garlic, minced	2	1	pkg (280 g) fish fillets, thawed, each cut in 3 pieces	1
1 cup	long-grain rice	250 mL			
1	bay leaf	1	1 cup	frozen peas	250 mL
1 tsp	finely chopped fresh oregano (or ¼ tsp/ 1 mL dried)	5 mL			

Cut sausage into ½-inch (1 cm) thick rounds. In large deep skillet or shallow wide saucepan, heat oil over medium heat; cook sausage until browned all over, about 10 minutes. Remove to drain.

Pour off all but 2 tbsp (25 mL) pan drippings. Add onions, red pepper and garlic to skillet; cook over medium heat for 3 to 5 minutes or until softened. Stir in rice and cook, stirring, until translucent, about 4 minutes. Add bay leaf, oregano, turmeric and pepper. Gradually stir in stock and bring to boil; reduce heat to medium-low and cook, covered, for 10 minutes. Push sausage rounds, clams, mussels (hinges down), and fish down into rice. Cover and simmer for about 10 minutes or until liquid has been absorbed, fish flakes easily with fork and shellfish have opened. Discard any shellfish that have not opened. Rinse peas well with hot water to thaw; stir into paella and let stand, covered, for 1 minute. Discard bay leaf.

*Instant seafood stock mix is available in delicatessens, but you might find it a little salty for this dish. Stock left over from poaching fish would be good instead.

Makes 4 servings.

Easy Family Paella
(page 48)

Crispy Fish and Chips
(page 49)

Hoisin Grilled Fillets
(page 50)

CRISPY FISH AND CHIPS

Fish and chips are undoubtedly an all-time favorite, and you won't find any lighter, crispier or less greasy than these. (Photograph opposite page.)

2 lb	baking potatoes (4 medium) Vegetable oil for deep-frying	1 kg	¼ cup	cornstarch	50 mL
			2 tsp	baking powder	10 mL
			1 tsp	granulated sugar	5 mL
1 lb	cod, haddock, turbot or perch fillets, thawed	500 g	½ tsp	salt	2 mL
				Pepper	
Batter:			¾ cup	water	175 mL
¾ cup	all-purpose flour	175 mL	1 tbsp	each vegetable oil and lemon juice	15 mL

Peel potatoes and cut into ½-inch (1 cm) thick strips, dropping them into bowl of ice water while you work. Drain well and spread on crumpled paper towels; pat thoroughly dry.

Pour enough oil into deep-fryer or heavy saucepan to come 3½ inches (9 cm) up sides of pan. For first deep-frying (there will be 2), heat oil until deep-frying thermometer registers 270°F (132°C); deep-fry potatoes, in 3 or 4 batches, for 3 to 5 minutes or until potatoes are tender and pale golden brown. Drain on crumpled paper towels and set aside for up to 1 hour before refrying.

Batter: Meanwhile, in mixing bowl, sift or stir together flour, cornstarch, baking powder, sugar, salt, and pepper to taste. Beat in water, oil and lemon juice, until well blended. Let stand at room temperature for 20 minutes.

Pat fish dry with paper towels; remove any skin if using perch. Swirl through batter, making sure pieces are well coated. Let all fish sit in batter for 5 minutes for batter to adhere better.

Heat oil in deep-fryer to 375°F (190°C); deep-fry fish, a few pieces at a time so that fish is not crowded, for about 4 minutes or until golden brown, turning pieces occasionally with spoon to prevent them from sticking together or to pan. Remove to shallow pan lined with crumpled paper towels; keep warm in 250°F (120°C) oven.

Heat oil to 385°F (196°C); deep-fry partially cooked potatoes, in 2 batches, shaking basket occasionally, for 2 to 4 minutes until potatoes are crisp and golden. Drain on crumpled paper towels. Heap fish in centre of large heated platter; surround with chips. Serve immediately.

Makes 4 servings.

HOISIN GRILLED FILLETS

Fish is naturally delicious on the grill where it absorbs the smokiness of the coals while retaining a fresh flavor and light texture. Here, a Chinese marinade adds an extra depth of flavor and color. (Photograph opposite page 49.)

2 tbsp	each dry sherry and rice vinegar*	25 mL	1	clove garlic, minced		1
1 tbsp	hoisin sauce*	15 mL	1 lb	cod or haddock fillets, thawed		500 g
1 tsp	each Oriental sesame oil and grated fresh gingerroot	5 mL		Green onion curls**		

In small bowl, combine sherry, vinegar, hoisin sauce, sesame oil, gingerroot and garlic. Pat fish dry with paper towels and place in shallow dish; spread hoisin mixture over top. Cover and refrigerate for at least 1 hour or up to 4 hours.

Place fillets on greased grill over medium-hot coals or at medium setting and grill for 4 to 8 minutes or until fish starts to flake with fork. Turn only thick pieces. Alternatively, broil 3 inches (8 cm) from heat for 4 to 8 minutes. Serve immediately garnished with green onion curls.

*Available in most supermarkets and specialty stores.

**To make green onion curls, cut green stems lengthwise into thin strips, being careful to leave green part attached to white parts; soak in ice water until curled.

Makes 4 servings.

HINTS FOR PERFECT GRILLED FISH

- The fish should be very cold, sometimes not even fully thawed, for best results.
- Be sure grill is clean.
- Oil grill and fish well.
- A fine wire basket is helpful to hold fillets; oil the inside.
- Turn only thick fillets; thin ones will cook through and are difficult to turn. Turn thick fillets with oiled spatula.
- Do not overcook. Pay close attention while fish cooks and remember it continues to cook for a moment after it's taken from grill.
- Place oiled spatula right under fillet to remove from grill.

Protein, a prime nutrient in seafood is essential for building and rebuilding body tissues. Ninety to ninety-six per cent of the protein in fish is digestible and contains all the amino acids needed for growth.

MICROWAVE FISH WITH TOMATO, HERBS AND LEMON

Iris Raven, a food writer who has a wonderful way with fish, discovered that these simple fresh ingredients contribute not only a subtle flavor to moist fish but also help produce a lemony sauce while everything cooks in the microwave. Serve with rice and spoon accumulated broth from cooked fish over the rice.

2 tbsp	butter, softened	25 mL	6	thin slices lemon	6
1 lb	haddock, cod or sole fillets, thawed	500 g	1	sprig each fresh thyme, basil and tarragon	1
	Pepper			Salt	
1	large firm ripe tomato, peeled, seeded and chopped	1			
Half	hot banana pepper, seeded and thinly sliced	Half			

Spread half of the butter on bottom of microwaveable shallow dish large enough to hold fillets in single layer. Arrange fillets in dish, with thickest parts toward outside and fold under very thin ends. Season with pepper to taste; dot with remaining butter.

Sprinkle tomato and banana pepper over fish. Arrange lemon slices over fillets; lay herb sprigs on top. Cover with waxed paper and microwave at medium-high (70%) power for 8 to 12 minutes or until fish flakes with fork. Remove lemon slices and herbs. Season with salt to taste.

Makes 3 or 4 servings.

COD AND ONIONS WITH BEER

Serve this simple dish with steamed green beans and boiled new potatoes for a quick and satisfying supper.

1 lb	cod fillets, thawed	500 g
	Salt and pepper	
¼ cup	butter	50 mL
3	onions, sliced (about 4 cups/1L)	3
Pinch	granulated sugar	Pinch

1 cup	beer	250 mL
1	bay leaf	1
¾ cup	fresh bread crumbs	175 mL
2 tbsp	butter, melted	25 mL
1 tbsp	chopped fresh parsley	15 mL

Pat fish dry with paper towels; sprinkle lightly with salt and pepper to taste. Set aside. In large skillet, melt butter over medium heat; cook onions and sugar for about 5 minutes or until onions are softened. Pour in beer and add bay leaf; increase heat to high and boil until liquid is reduced by about one-third, about 4 minutes. Discard bay leaf.

Spread onion mixture in shallow baking dish just big enough to hold fillets in single layer; lay fillets on top.

In small bowl, stir together bread crumbs, butter and parsley; sprinkle evenly over fish. Bake uncovered in 400°F (200°C) oven for about 20 minutes or until fish flakes with fork and topping is crisp.

Makes 3 or 4 servings.

PEANUT CRUNCH OVEN-FRIED FILLETS

An easy coating adds crunch to fish while keeping it moist inside. Accompany with Oven-baked Potato Slices (see page 39) and creamy coleslaw. If using salted peanuts, reduce the amount of salt called for in the recipe.

1	pkg (280 g) fish fillets, thawed	1	½ tsp	salt	2 mL
			¼ tsp	pepper	1 mL
½ cup	fine dry bread crumbs	125 mL	1	egg, beaten	1
¼ cup	finely chopped peanuts	50 mL	2 tsp	vegetable oil	10 mL

Pat fish very dry with paper towels; set aside. In shallow dish, stir together bread crumbs, peanuts, salt and pepper. In another bowl, beat together egg and oil. Dip each fish fillet into egg mixture, then into crumbs; place on greased baking sheet. (Recipe can be prepared ahead to this point, covered and refrigerated up to 6 hours.)

Bake, uncovered, in 450°F (230°C) oven for 6 minutes. Turn and bake for 2 to 3 minutes longer or until crispy and fish flakes with fork.

Makes 2 or 3 servings.

VARIATIONS:

Almond Crunch Oven-fried Sole Fillets

Substitute finely chopped almonds for the peanuts and use sole fillets.

Sesame Crunch Oven-fried Fillets

Substitute 2 tbsp (25 mL) sesame seeds for the peanuts.

Pan-fried Fillets

If desired, you can coat fillets as above and pan-fry. Melt enough shortening over medium heat to cover bottom of skillet to depth of ⅛ inch (3 mm). Cook fillets for 3 minutes per side or until crisp and golden and fish flakes with fork. (The Sesame Crunch Fillets are especially good pan-fried.)

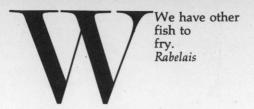

W We have other
fish to
fry.
Rabelais

FISH STICKS

If you're serving these to company, call them
"goujons"; if you're serving them to the local gang,
call them fish sticks or fingers. Whatever you call
them, they're sure to be a hit. Serve them with
Tartar Sauce (page 80), Thousand Island Sauce
(page 85) or a flavored mayonnaise (page 83).

1 lb	fish fillets (cod, haddock or sole), thawed	500 g	¼ cup	milk	50 mL	
⅓ cup	all-purpose flour	75 mL	1⅓ cups	finely ground cracker crumbs (about 36)	325 mL	
¼ tsp	salt	1 mL		Vegetable oil for deep-frying		
Pinch	pepper	Pinch		Lemon wedges		
1	egg	1				

Cut each fillet in half crosswise; cut each half lengthwise into 3 or 4 narrow strips. Pat very dry with paper towels.

In shallow bowl or on waxed paper, combine flour, salt and pepper. In another shallow bowl, beat egg lightly; blend in milk. Place cracker crumbs on waxed paper. Coat each fish piece thoroughly with seasoned flour, shaking off excess. Dip into egg mixture, then into cracker crumbs to coat. (Fish can be coated ahead, placed in single layer on large plate, covered with waxed paper and refrigerated for up to 6 hours.)

Pour oil into deep-fryer or large saucepan to depth of about 3½ inches (9 cm); heat until deep-fryer thermometer registers 375°F (190°C). Fry fish, in batches, for 2 to 3 minutes or until crisp and golden brown. Drain on crumpled paper towels in shallow baking dish. Keep warm in 250°F (120°C) oven while frying rest. Serve immediately garnished with lemon wedges.

Makes 3 or 4 servings.

Fish is valued because it contains a high proportion (more than beef or pork) of Omega-3 fatty acids. Omega-3 is believed to have positive effects on blood vessels and may reduce the risk of heart disease.

QUICK CURRIED FILLETS

Serve this easy skillet supper with steamed rice and green peas or beans. There's enough sauce for 1 lb (500 g) fish if you want to serve 3 or 4 people.

2 tbsp	butter	25 mL	¼ tsp	salt	1 mL
1 tbsp	curry powder	15 mL	1	pkg (280 g) fish fillets, thawed	1
¼ cup	finely chopped peeled apple	50 mL	¼ cup	coarsely chopped toasted cashews or peanuts	50 mL
1	small onion, chopped	1	2 tbsp	sliced green onions	25 mL
1	small clove garlic, minced	1			
½ cup	whipping cream	125 mL			

In large skillet, melt butter over low heat; stir in curry powder until dissolved. Add apple, onion and garlic; cook, stirring, for 2 minutes. Stir in cream and salt; simmer over medium heat for 1 to 2 minutes or until slightly thickened. Add fillets; cover and cook for 3 to 5 minutes or until fish flakes with fork. Serve sprinkled with toasted nuts and green onions.

Makes 2 or 3 servings.

T Take an old grill, three feet high,
twisted by ancient fires, lay the
fish upon it, baptize it with the sauce,
and plant the whole thing in the
middle of your fiery inferno.
Prisons et Paradis, Colette

GRILLED FISH FAJITAS

Refreshing tomato salsa and creamy guacamole
coat moist grilled fish rolled inside warm flour
tortillas for an easy, fun and quick supper.

1 lb	fish fillets, thawed	500 g		**Guacamole:**		
4	flour tortillas	4		1	ripe avocado	1
	Fresh Tomato Salsa			¼ cup	chopped red onion	50 mL
	(page 85)			2 tbsp	lime juice	25 mL
⅓ cup	plain yogurt or sour	75 mL		1 tbsp	finely chopped fresh	15 mL
	cream				coriander	
	Fresh coriander sprigs			1 tbsp	minced fresh or	15 mL
Marinade:					canned jalapeño	
¼ cup	lime juice	50 mL			pepper	
2 tbsp	vegetable oil	25 mL		¼ tsp	salt	1 mL
1	clove garlic, minced	1		Pinch	ground cumin	Pinch
¼ tsp	hot pepper flakes	1 mL				
Pinch	dried oregano	Pinch				

Pat fillets very dry with paper towels;
place in shallow glass bowl.

Marinade: In small bowl, stir together
lime juice, oil, garlic, hot pepper
flakes and oregano; pour over fish.
Cover and refrigerate for 1 hour, turning
occasionally.

Guacamole: In small bowl, mash
avocado; blend in onion, lime juice,
coriander, jalapeño pepper, salt and
cumin.

Assembly: Warm tortillas on grill,
turning often. (Or, if broiling fish, wrap
tortillas in foil and warm in oven while
preheating it and broiling fish.)

Place fish on well-oiled grill over
medium-hot coals or at medium setting;
grill for 4 to 8 minutes or until fish flakes
with fork, turning only thicker pieces.
(Alternatively, broil 3½ inches/9 cm
from heat.) Remove fish to board with
oiled spatula; slice thinly or flake in
large pieces.

Place warmed tortilla on each plate.
Evenly divide fish and arrange down
centre of each tortilla. Top each evenly
with guacamole, Fresh Tomato Salsa
and yogurt, leaving a little guacamole to
drizzle over folded tortillas. Fold up
each tortilla to enclose mixture; evenly drizzle remaining guacamole on centre of each. Garnish with sprigs of
coriander.

Makes 4 servings.

C Cod has that splendid virtue of nonassertiveness that makes the palate revel in things with which it is bedded or topped, including noodles, spinach, cheese, sauces or . . . melted butter. . . . *Craig Claiborne's Favorites from The New York Times, Craig Claiborne, Times Books, 1976.*

BAKED COD GREEK STYLE

Colorful and full of flavor, this easy oven supper is great with rice and a crisp green salad.

1 lb	cod fillets, thawed or partially thawed	500 g	2 tbsp	minced fresh parsley	25 mL
	Salt and pepper		1½ tsp	chopped fresh oregano (or ½ tsp/ 2 mL dried)	7 mL
2 tbsp	olive oil	25 mL			
1	sweet green pepper, cut in ½-inch (1 cm) strips	1	Pinch	each hot pepper flakes and granulated sugar	Pinch
18	pitted black olives	18	¼ lb	drained feta cheese, crumbled (about 1 cup/250 mL)	125 g
1	onion, finely chopped	1			
3	cloves garlic, minced	3			
1	can (19 oz/540 mL) tomatoes (undrained)	1			

Arrange fish in single layer in greased baking dish. Sprinkle lightly with salt and pepper to taste.

In large skillet, heat oil over medium-high heat; cook green pepper, olives, onion and garlic for 3 to 5 minutes or until onion and garlic are softened. Stir in tomatoes, parsley, oregano, hot pepper flakes and sugar. Reduce heat to medium and cook, uncovered and stirring, for 5 minutes. Spoon over fish; sprinkle with feta and bake, uncovered, in 375°F (190°C) oven for 15 to 18 minutes for thawed, 20 to 25 minutes for partially thawed fillets, or until fish flakes with fork.

Makes 4 servings.

STIR-FRIED COD WITH PEPPERS AND CASHEWS

Serve this quick, colorful supper on hot rice or Chinese noodles. Use one whole pepper of any color instead of this combination, if you wish. In our cover photograph, small-leafed (bush) basil was used as a garnish.

1 lb	cod or haddock fillets, thawed	500 g	1	clove garlic, minced	1
1	egg white	1	2 tbsp	soy sauce	25 mL
1 tbsp	dry sherry or rice wine	15 mL	1 tsp	granulated sugar	5 mL
2 tbsp	cornstarch	25 mL	Pinch	hot pepper flakes	Pinch
¼ tsp	salt	1 mL	¼ cup	(approx) peanut or vegetable oil	50 mL
Half	each sweet red and green pepper	Half	¼ cup	cashew pieces or peanuts	50 mL
2	stalks celery	2			
2 tsp	minced or grated fresh gingerroot	10 mL			

Cut fish fillets lengthwise into 1½-inch (4 cm) wide strips; cut across into 2½-inch (6 cm) lengths. Press between paper towels to dry well. In large pie plate, whisk egg white slightly; whisk in sherry. Stir in cornstarch and salt. Toss fish pieces in mixture, coating well. Set aside.

Seed and cut red and green peppers diagonally into ¾-inch (2 cm) wide strips. Cut celery diagonally into ½-inch (1 cm) wide strips. Place peppers and celery in bowl or on waxed paper along with gingerroot and garlic; set aside. In small bowl, stir together soy sauce, sugar and hot pepper flakes; set aside.

In wok or large skillet, heat 2 tbsp (25 mL) of the oil over medium-high heat; stir-fry pepper mixture for 2 minutes. With slotted spoon, transfer to warm platter. Add sufficient oil to pan to make about 3 tbsp (45 mL); heat for 30 seconds. Stir-fry fish for 2 minutes or just until opaque. Return pepper mixture to pan; add soy sauce mixture and nuts and stir-fry for 1 minute. Serve immediately on warm plates.

Makes 4 servings.

EASY ENTERTAINING

Frozen fish fillets are an unexpectedly easy way to entertain elegantly. But just because some of these recipes may take slightly longer to prepare or have an upscale presentation, don't overlook them when planning a special dinner for the family.

Some of the dishes are complete suppers in themselves while others require only a simple accompaniment such as steamed rice, mashed potatoes, couscous or polenta along with a green salad or fresh vegetable.

DEEP-DISH SEAFOOD PIE

This is a good old-fashioned standby for easy entertaining since everyone will love the creamy seafood mixture under its flaky topping. But, better yet, you can make it all in advance.

2 tbsp	butter	25 mL	½ lb	shrimp, peeled and deveined	250 g
1	onion, coarsely chopped	1	1 cup	frozen peas	250 mL
2	stalks celery, coarsely chopped	2	½ cup	whipping cream	125 mL
2	carrots, in ½-inch (1 cm) chunks	2	¼ cup	chopped fresh parsley	50 mL
3 tbsp	all-purpose flour	50 mL	1½ tsp	lemon juice	7 mL
1 cup	fish stock*	250 mL	½ tsp	salt	2 mL
¼ cup	dry white wine or additional stock	50 mL	¼ tsp	pepper	1 mL
1½ tsp	each fresh thyme and savory (or ½ tsp/2 mL each crushed dried)	7 mL	Half	pkg (14 oz/397 g) frozen puff pastry, thawed	Half
1 lb	fish fillets, thawed	500 g		1 egg yolk mixed with 1 tbsp (15 mL) cold water	

In large heavy saucepan, melt butter over medium heat; cook onion, celery and carrots, stirring occasionally, for about 5 minutes or until onions are softened. Sprinkle with flour and cook, stirring for 2 minutes. Stir in stock, wine, thyme and savory. (Mixture will be quite thick.) Bring to boil and reduce heat; cover and simmer over very low heat for 10 minutes or until carrots are tender-crisp, stirring occasionally. Let cool to room temperature.

Pat fish dry with paper towels; cut into 2-inch (5 cm) pieces. Stir fish, shrimp, peas, cream, parsley, lemon juice, salt and pepper into cream mixture. Spoon into 7-cup (1.75 L) ovenproof casserole or baking dish that's about 2 inches (5 cm) deep and 9 inches (23 cm) wide. (Recipe can be prepared ahead to this point, covered and refrigerated for up to 8 hours.)

On lightly floured surface, roll out pastry to ⅛-inch (3 mm) thickness to fit over top of baking dish. Brush underside of pastry lightly with egg yolk mixture and place over fish mixture, pressing edges of pastry to dish without stretching pastry. Cut decorative fish shapes out of any scraps. (Pie and pastry shapes can be prepared to this point and refrigerated for up to 2 hours.) Reserve remaining egg yolk mixture.

Cut hole in centre of pastry for steam to escape. Brush top with egg wash; arrange pastry cut-outs decoratively on top and brush with egg wash. Bake in 400°F (200°C) oven for 10 to 12 minutes or until pastry is golden. Reduce temperature to 375°F (190°C) and bake for another 20 minutes.

*Instant seafood stock mix is available in delicatessens.

Makes about 6 servings.

PESTO BAKED FILLETS AND POTATOES

Accompany this fresh-tasting main course with corn on the cob or baked squash for a wonderful harvest celebration meal. Serve as family or company fare.

4	potatoes (unpeeled)	4		Pepper		
3 tbsp	butter, melted	50 mL	2 tbsp	freshly grated	25 mL
1 lb	fish fillets, thawed	500 g		Parmesan cheese	
½ cup	Pesto Sauce (page 90)	125 mL	1 tbsp	dry bread crumbs	15 mL
1	large tomato, peeled, seeded and diced	1			

Scrub potatoes and slice as thinly as possible. Bring large saucepan of salted water to boil; add potatoes and cook for 5 minutes. Drain well in sieve and toss with butter.

Arrange fillets in shallow baking dish just big enough to hold them in single layer. Place prepared potato slices around and over fillets. Spread Pesto Sauce over all. Sprinkle with tomato, and lots of black pepper to taste.

In small bowl, stir together Parmesan and bread crumbs; sprinkle evenly over top. Bake, uncovered, in 400°F (200°C) oven for about 20 minutes or until fish flakes with fork.

Makes 3 or 4 servings.

SOLE AND VEGETABLES BAKED IN PARCHMENT

This time-honored treatment of fish called *en papillote* is perfect for an elegant dinner. Let guests open their own packages (which you can prepare well in advance) to welcome the inviting aroma and colorful sight of freshly cooked fish and vegetables. Vary the vegetables and use your favorites or what you have on hand. Just remember to cut them so that they cook in the same amount of time. For a romantic dinner for two, just halve the recipe.

1 lb	sole fillets, thawed	500 g	1	tomato, peeled, seeded and diced	1
	Salt and pepper				
3 tbsp	butter, melted	50 mL	2 tsp	finely chopped fresh tarragon (or ½ tsp/ 2 mL crushed dried)	10 mL
1	small zucchini, thinly sliced	1			
4	large mushrooms, sliced	4	¼ cup	dry vermouth or dry white wine	50 mL
1	leek, slivered (white part only)	1			

Pat fillets very dry with paper towels; sprinkle lightly with salt and pepper to taste.

Cut 4 sheets of parchment paper or foil about 18 × 15 inches (45 × 38 cm). Fold each piece in half lengthwise, then cut each piece into a half-heart shape, as you would a valentine. Unfold and brush lightly with some of the melted butter; set remaining butter aside.

Layer one fourth of the fish and vegetables on one half of each heart, starting with fish, then zucchini, mushrooms, leek and tomato. Sprinkle each with one-fourth of the tarragon; drizzle with one-fourth of the vermouth.

Drizzle each evenly with remaining butter; sprinkle lightly with salt and pepper to taste.

Fold other half of each heart over fish and vegetables and bring cut edges of paper together. Seal each package by starting at rounded top and making series of small tight overlapping folds. Transfer packages to 2 baking sheets. If using parchment paper, packages can be prepared ahead and refrigerated for up to 8 hours. If using foil packages, refrigerate for only 1 hour.

Bake in 425°F (220°C) oven for 15 minutes. To serve, have each guest cut package in a cross to open.

Makes 4 servings.

VARIATION:

Pesto Papillotes

1 lb	cod or haddock fish fillets, thawed	500 g
⅓ cup	Pesto Sauce (page 90)	75 mL
4	thin lemon slices	4

Prepare parchment paper and fish as above; spread Pesto Sauce evenly over each fillet. Top each with lemon slice and fold each package as above; bake for 12 minutes.

The cooking of fish . . . is one of the easiest of all forms of cookery. In a sautéed fish recipe . . . the fillets once cooked, may be served as is or, even better . . . with a mustard hollandaise.
Cooking with Craig Claiborne and Pierre Franey, Craig Claiborne and Pierre Franey, Fawcett Columbine, 1983.

LEMON AND VERMOUTH SAUTÉED SOLE

Steamed rice and broccoli or asparagus are good accompaniments for this quick fish sauté with its lemony sauce.

1 lb	sole fillets, thawed	500 g	1 tsp	grated lemon rind	5 mL
2 tbsp	all-purpose flour	25 mL	3 tbsp	vegetable oil	50 mL
¼ tsp	each salt and white pepper	1 mL	1	stalk celery, finely chopped	1
¼ cup	lemon juice	50 mL	2	green onions, chopped	2
1 tbsp	granulated sugar	15 mL			
1 tbsp	dry vermouth or white wine	15 mL			

Cut sole into 2-inch (5 cm) squares; pat very dry with paper towels. In shallow bowl, stir together flour, salt and pepper. Coat fish lightly with flour mixture. Set aside.

In small saucepan, stir together lemon juice, sugar, vermouth and lemon rind. Cook over medium-low heat until reduced by half, 2 to 3 minutes. Remove from heat and set aside to keep warm.

In large skillet or wok, heat 1 tbsp (15 mL) of the oil over medium-high heat; stir-fry celery for 45 seconds. Add remaining oil, green onions and fish; cook, stirring, for 2 to 3 minutes or until fish is opaque. Serve immediately with lemon sauce poured over top.

Makes about 4 servings.

Fish does not receive the full measure of gastronomic recognition that it deserves.
A Concise Encyclopedia of Gastronomy, André L. Simone, The Overlook Press, 1981.

HERB-STUFFED FILLETS BAKED IN PASTRY

Perfect for a dinner party, these elegantly wrapped fish fillets can be prepared ahead.

8	fish fillets, thawed (each about 5 × 3 inches/12 × 8 cm)	8
2 tbsp	unsalted butter	25 mL
2 tbsp	finely chopped shallots (or onion)	25 mL
¼ cup	finely chopped fresh parsley	50 mL
¼ cup	snipped fresh chives	50 mL
2 tbsp	finely chopped fresh summer savory (or 1½ tsp/7 mL dried)	25 mL
2 tbsp	finely chopped fresh marjoram (or 1½ tsp/ 7 mL dried)	25 mL
2 tbsp	lemon juice	25 mL
1 tsp	paprika	5 mL
½ tsp	salt	2 mL
	Pepper	
1	pkg (16 oz/454 g) phyllo pastry*	1
1 cup	unsalted butter, melted	250 mL
	Hollandaise Sauce (pages 86/87)	

Pat fish dry with paper towel; cut 4 diagonal slits ½ inch (1 cm) deep in each fillet.

In small saucepan, melt 2 tbsp (25 mL) butter over medium heat; cook shallots for 3 minutes or until softened. Remove to small bowl and stir in parsley, chives, savory, marjoram, lemon juice, paprika, salt, and pepper to taste; mix well. Stuff equal amounts of herb mixture into slits in fillets. Pat fish dry again.

Unwrap phyllo and count sheets to allow equal number of sheets to wrap each fillet (average package has 24 sheets). Cut stack of sheets in half crosswise. Cover pastry with waxed paper and damp tea towel to keep it moist while you work.

Using 6 half-sheets for each fillet, brush 1 sheet with some of the melted butter. Place second sheet on top and brush evenly with butter. Repeat with remaining 4 sheets. Place 1 stuffed fillet lengthwise on top of stack; fold long sides of phyllo over fish; then fold over narrow ends to seal. Transfer wrapped fillet, seam side down, to ungreased baking sheet; brush top and sides with melted butter. Repeat with remaining pastry and fish. (Fish can be prepared ahead to this point, covered and refrigerated for up to 6 hours.)

Bake in 375°F (190°C) oven for about 25 minutes or until pastry is golden brown at edges and pale brown in centre. Serve immediately with Hollandaise Sauce.

*Phyllo, or filo, pastry is available in the freezer section of most supermarkets.

Makes 8 servings.

Fish Salad
Niçoise
(page 73)

Curried Fish Salad
with Mango Mayonnaise
Dressing
(page 74)

Fresh Tomato Salsa
(page 85)

The early growth of Nova Scotia, Newfoundland, and New England was based on neither furs nor bullion, but on the mighty cod.

Development of Nova Scotia's Fishing Fleet, Nova Scotia Department of Fisheries, 1979.

COD AND TOMATO CUSTARD

This subtly flavored fish casserole is an excellent focus for a brunch, accompanied by rice and a marinated vegetable salad.

2	pkg (each 280 g) cod fillets, frozen	2
3¼ cups	milk	800 mL
1	onion, minced	1
2	cloves garlic, minced	2
1	bay leaf	1
¼ cup	butter	50 mL
¼ cup	all-purpose flour	50 mL
½ tsp	salt	2 mL
½ tsp	dry mustard	2 mL
¼ tsp	(approx) pepper	1 mL
5	tomatoes, peeled and sliced	5
2	eggs	2
1 cup	shredded old Cheddar cheese (about ¼ lb/125 g)	250 mL
2 tbsp	butter	25 mL

Place fillets in deep skillet and pour in 2 cups (500 mL) of the milk; add onion, garlic and bay leaf. Bring slowly to boil; cover and reduce heat; simmer for about 7 to 10 minutes or until fish flakes easily with fork. Drain, reserving milk mixture. Discard bay leaf. Flake cod into greased 9-inch (2.5 L) square baking dish.

In heavy saucepan, melt ¼ cup (50 mL) butter over medium heat; add flour and cook, stirring, without browning, for 2 minutes. Remove from heat and gradually whisk in warm reserved milk.

Return to medium heat and cook, stirring, until thickened and smooth. Stir in salt, mustard and pepper.

Pour sauce over fish; cover with tomato slices in single layer. Sprinkle generously with pepper. (Recipe can be prepared ahead to this point, covered and refrigerated for up to 4 hours.)

In medium bowl, beat together eggs, cheese and remaining 1¼ cups (300 mL) milk; pour over tomatoes. Dot with 2 tbsp (25 mL) butter. Bake uncovered, in 325°F (160°C) oven for about 45 minutes or until golden brown.

Makes 6 servings.

SOLE ROLL-UPS WITH
GARLIC-HERB FILLING OR
SPINACH-TARRAGON FILLING

Drizzle these pretty roll-ups with a creamy sauce like Hollandaise or Cream Sauce (pages 87/89) for an impressive but simple company meal. Here are two fillings to try, but use your imagination for more, depending on what you have in the house. Each filling is enough for 1 pound (500 g) of fillets.

1 lb	sole fillets, thawed	500 g
Garlic-Herb Filling:		
2 tbsp	butter	25 mL
2	green onions, chopped	2
1	clove garlic, minced	1
½ cup	fresh bread crumbs	125 mL
¼ cup	chopped fresh parsley	50 mL
2 tbsp	snipped fresh dill (or 2 tsp/10 mL dried dillweed)	25 mL
2 tbsp	lemon juice	25 mL
	Salt and pepper	

Pat fillets dry with paper towels; halve any that are large or have been butterflied. Set aside.

Garlic-Herb Filling: In medium skillet, melt half of the butter over medium heat; cook onions and garlic until soft, about 2 minutes. Remove from heat; stir in bread crumbs, parsley, dill, half of the lemon juice, and salt and pepper to taste.

Sprinkle crumb mixture evenly over fillets. Starting at thin end, loosely roll up each jelly-roll style and secure with toothpicks. Arrange seam-side down in buttered 8-inch (2 L) square baking dish. Season lightly with salt and pepper. In small pan, heat remaining butter and lemon juice just until butter melts; drizzle over rolls. Bake, uncovered, in 400°F (200°C) oven for about 15 minutes or until fish flakes with fork.

Makes 4 servings.

VARIATION:
Spinach-Tarragon Filling

2 tbsp	butter	25 mL
2	green onions, thinly sliced	2
Half	pkg (10 oz/284 g) spinach (about 4 cups/1 L)	Half
⅓ cup	fine dry bread crumbs	75 mL
2 tsp	finely chopped fresh tarragon (or ½ tsp/ 2 mL dried)	10 mL
¼ tsp	grated lemon rind	1 mL
	Salt and pepper	
1 tbsp	lemon juice	15 mL

In skillet, melt half the butter over medium-low heat; cook onions for 2 minutes or until softened. Meanwhile, wash spinach and shake off excess water; trim and tear coarsely. With just water clinging to leaves, add to skillet; increase heat to medium-high and cook, stirring, until spinach is wilted and only about 1 tbsp (15 mL) liquid remains in pan. Remove from heat; stir in bread crumbs, tarragon, lemon rind, and salt and pepper to taste. Spread about 2 tbsp (25 mL) of mixture on dried fillets. Continue with recipe as above.

Microwave Method:
Arrange in microwave-proof dish; season with pepper but not salt. Pour butter-lemon mixture over top and cover with waxed paper; microwave at High for 5 to 8 minutes or until fish flakes with fork.

After a good dinner, one can forgive anybody, even one's own relations.
Oscar Wilde

FISH FONDUE

Fondues come and go in popularity, but they are always fun for casual entertaining. If you have two fondue pots, use one at each end of the table, since the fish cooks better if it isn't too crowded.

2 lb	ocean perch fillets, thawed	1 kg
	Salt and pepper	
	Parsley sprigs	
	Lemon wedges	
	Peanut or vegetable oil for deep-frying	
	Tartar Sauce (page 80) or Mustard Mayonnaise (page 83)	

Batter:		
2	eggs, separated	2
1 cup	beer or milk	250 mL
1 tbsp	peanut or vegetable oil	15 mL
1 cup	all-purpose flour	250 mL
¼ tsp	salt	1 mL
Pinch	granulated sugar	Pinch

Batter: In medium bowl, beat together egg yolks, beer and oil. Sift or stir together flour, salt and sugar; gradually add to liquid ingredients, stirring just until blended. Cover and let stand at room temperature for 1 hour or in refrigerator overnight. Reserve egg whites until just before serving time.

Remove skin from fish and cut into 1-inch (2.5 cm) pieces; divide among 6 serving plates. Lightly season with salt and pepper to taste; garnish plates with parsley and lemon.

In fondue pot on stove, heat oil to about 375°F (190°C) or until 1-inch (2.5 cm) cube of white bread turns golden brown in 50 seconds. Place fondue burner on very thick heatproof pad in centre of table; transfer pot of hot oil to burner. Keep heat high.

Meanwhile, beat egg whites until stiff but not dry peaks form; fold into batter. Pour into several small bowls around table. Using fondue forks, guests can dip fish pieces into batter, then deep-fry in oil for 5 minutes or until brown. Serve hot with Tartar Sauce or Mustard Mayonnaise.

Makes 6 servings.

FISH RISOTTO

This inexpensive main course is quick to make and very appealing with a tomato salad and crusty whole wheat rolls.

1	pkg (280 g) cod fillets, thawed	1
¼ cup	butter	50 mL
2 tbsp	olive or vegetable oil	25 mL
1	onion, diced	1
3½ cups	(approx) chicken broth	875 mL
1⅓ cups	short-grain rice, preferably Italian arborio	325 mL
1 cup	frozen peas	250 mL
¼ cup	chopped fresh parsley	50 mL
¼ cup	freshly grated Parmesan cheese	50 mL
	Salt and pepper	

Pat fillets dry with paper towels; cut into 1½-inch (4 cm) pieces. Set aside.

In large saucepan, melt half of the butter with oil over low heat; cook onion until golden, about 15 minutes.

Meanwhile, in small saucepan, heat chicken broth until hot; keep hot over very low heat.

Add rice to onion in large saucepan; increase heat to medium and cook, stirring constantly, for about 5 minutes or until edges of grains are transparent. Pour enough hot broth into rice mixture to cover by ¼ inch (5 mm). Adjust heat to maintain good simmer; simmer, stirring constantly, for about 5 minutes or until liquid is absorbed and you can see bottom of pan when stirring. Add more broth to cover as before and continue to simmer, stirring constantly, until liquid is absorbed. Repeat, adding broth and simmering until rice is tender but still slightly firm in centre. Add fish for last 2 minutes simmering. Rinse peas with hot water to thaw; stir into rice mixture along with remaining butter. Stir in parsley, cheese, and salt and pepper to taste. Heat through. Taste and adjust seasoning.

Makes about 4 servings.

 Lean fish such as sole, cod and haddock are low in calories and cholesterol content, having a fat content of no more than 5% and frequently less than 2%.

SOLE IN LETTUCE PACKAGES

No one will ever be able to guess how few calories there are in these delicious fish and vegetable bundles baked in white wine. (Photograph opposite page 33.)

1 lb	sole fillets, thawed	500 g
½ cup	dry white wine	125 mL
1	large head iceberg lettuce	1
1 cup	sliced mushrooms (¼ lb/125 g)	250 mL
½ cup	sliced water chestnuts	125 mL
4	shallots, chopped	4
2	carrots, thinly sliced	2
1 cup	low-salt chicken stock	250 mL

In shallow dish, marinate sole in wine for 20 minutes. With slotted spoon, remove fish and set aside, reserving wine.

Remove core from lettuce; carefully remove each leaf, making 4 piles of 4 leaves each, with larger leaves on bottom. (Don't worry if a leaf rips; just arrange each pile so that hole is covered by next leaf.) Arrange one-quarter of the fish on top of each lettuce pile. Divide mushrooms, water chestnuts, shallots and carrots into 4 portions and arrange on top of fish. Wrap lettuce around fish and vegetables; tie with string in criss-cross fashion.

Arrange lettuce packages in single layer in large baking dish or small roaster. Combine stock and reserved wine; pour over packages. Cover tightly and bake in 375°F (190°C) oven for 20 minutes or until heated through. With slotted spoon, remove packages to heated platter and serve immediately.

Makes 4 servings.

GRILLED TARRAGON-LEMON SOLE

This is the type of fast, inviting dish you will enjoy making after a hard day at work. Grill some mushroom caps alongside and toss a refreshing green salad with lots of tomato wedges.

1	pkg (280 g) sole fillets, thawed	1	1 tsp	grated lemon rind	5 mL
2 tbsp	butter, melted	25 mL	2 tbsp	lemon juice	25 mL
2 tsp	chopped fresh tarragon (or ½ tsp/2 mL dried)	10 mL		Tarragon sprigs (optional) Lemon slices	

Poke several holes in large piece of greased foil. Pat fish very dry with paper towels. Brush both sides of fillets with most of the melted butter; arrange in single layer on foil. Sprinkle with chopped tarragon and lemon rind. Place foil on grill 4 inches (10 cm) above medium-hot coals or on medium-high setting. Cook for about 4 minutes or until fish begins to flake with fork, brushing with remaining butter as it cooks. Do not turn. Sprinkle with lemon juice and garnish with tarragon sprigs and lemon slices to serve.

Makes 2 or 3 servings.

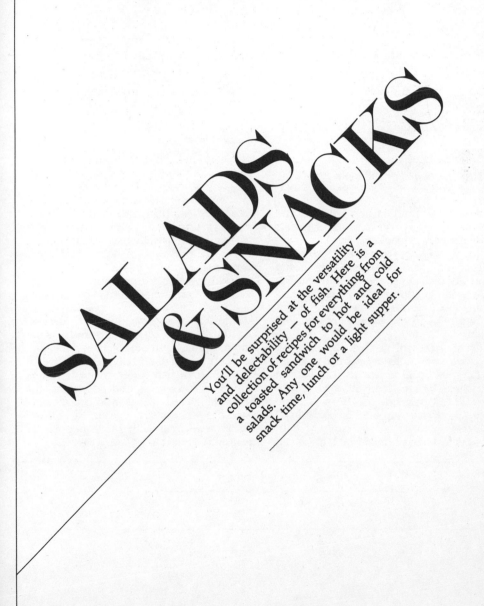

SALADS & SNACKS

You'll be surprised at the versatility — and delectability — of fish. Here is a collection of recipes for everything from a toasted sandwich to hot and cold salads. Any one would be ideal for snack time, lunch or a light supper.

CAESAR'S SOLE

Ocean perch is quite good in this crunchy salad, but I couldn't resist the pun.

1	large head romaine lettuce	1
6	slices French bread	6
1	pkg (280 g) sole or ocean perch fillets, thawed	1
1 tbsp	olive oil	15 mL
	Salt and pepper	

Dressing:

3	cloves garlic	3
1 tbsp	balsamic or red wine vinegar	15 mL
¼ tsp	Dijon mustard	1 mL
	Salt and pepper	
¼ cup	olive oil	50 mL
1½ tsp	Worcestershire sauce	7 mL
½ tsp	anchovy paste	2 mL
1	egg (unshelled)	1
1 tbsp	lemon juice	15 mL
⅓ cup	freshly grated Parmesan cheese	75 mL

Wash, dry and tear lettuce into bite-sized pieces. Wrap in paper towels and refrigerate in plastic bag.

Remove crusts from bread; cut bread into ½-inch (1 cm) cubes. (You should have about 2 cups/500 mL.) Spread on baking sheet and broil 4 inches (10 cm) from heat, turning once, for about 2 minutes or until evenly toasted. Set aside.

Brush fish with 1 tbsp (15 mL) oil; sprinkle with salt and pepper to taste. Arrange in broiling pan and broil about 4 inches (10 cm) from heat for about 3 minutes per side or until opaque throughout, turning once if possible.

Dressing: Cut 1 garlic clove in half; rub cut side over inside of large salad bowl. Crush all the garlic and place in bowl. Whisk in vinegar, mustard, and salt and pepper to taste. Gradually whisk in oil. Stir in Worcestershire sauce and anchovy paste.

Coddle egg by dipping into boiling water for 45 seconds. Place in cold water to cool. Set aside.

Add lettuce to bowl; toss with dressing until leaves glisten. Sprinkle with lemon juice and toss again. Break coddled egg onto salad and toss well. Cut or break fish fillets crosswise into ½-inch (1 cm) strips and add to bowl. Sprinkle bread cubes and Parmesan cheese over top; toss again. Taste and adjust seasoning with more pepper if desired. Serve immediately.

Makes 4 servings.

What an idiot is man to believe that abstaining from flesh, and eating fish, which is so much more delicate and delicious, constitutes fasting.
Napoleon

FISH SALAD NIÇOISE

This attractive main-course salad will soon become a favorite on warm summer evenings. (Photograph opposite page 64.)

1 lb	fish fillets, frozen	500 g
6	potatoes (or 12 small)	6
¾ lb	green beans	375 g
Half	small red onion	Half
Half	each sweet red and yellow pepper	Half
¾ cup	pitted black olives	175 mL
3	tomatoes	3
3	hard-cooked eggs	3
1	small head romaine lettuce	1
2 tbsp	chopped fresh parsley	25 mL

Dressing:		
1	egg	1
2 tbsp	white wine vinegar	25 mL
1 tbsp	chopped fresh basil (or 1 tsp/5mL dried)	15 mL
1 tbsp	lemon juice	15 mL
1	clove garlic, minced	1
2 tsp	Dijon mustard	10 mL
½ tsp	pepper	2 mL
½ tsp	salt	2 mL
½ tsp	anchovy paste	2 mL
¾ cup	olive oil	175 mL

Dressing: In small bowl, whisk together egg, vinegar, basil, lemon juice, garlic, mustard, pepper, salt and anchovy paste. Gradually whisk in oil. (Dressing can be made ahead, covered and refrigerated for up to 1 day; whisk again before using.)

Cut frozen fish into 1½-inch (4 cm) pieces; poach for about 7 to 10 minutes or until fish flakes with fork. (See page 10 for poaching technique.) Drain well and set aside.

Cook potatoes in small amount of boiling salted water until tender; drain well. Cut small potatoes in half and larger ones into quarters. Place in bowl and add half of the dressing; toss to combine while potatoes are hot. Set aside to let cool.

Trim beans and cook in large pot of boiling water, until just tender, 4 to 5 minutes. Drain and refresh under cold running water. Wrap in clean tea towel and set aside. (Refrigerate if leaving for more than 1 hour.)

Thinly slice onion; cut peppers into wide strips. Add onion, peppers, fish and olives to potatoes. Toss gently to coat with dressing. (Recipe can be prepared ahead to this point, covered and refrigerated up to 8 hours.)

Cut each tomato into 6 wedges. Peel eggs; quarter lengthwise. Arrange lettuce leaves in fan shape on large platter; mound potato mixture over stem ends. Arrange tomato and egg wedges along edges; tuck in green beans. Garnish with parsley and drizzle with remaining dressing.

Makes 6 servings.

CURRIED FISH SALAD WITH
MANGO MAYONNAISE DRESSING

Mango chutney is available in most supermarkets and lends a unique sweetness to this delightful salad. In our photograph facing page 64, the salad has been garnished with sliced mangoes and lightly coated with mango mayonnaise dressing.

1 lb	ocean perch, partially thawed or cod/haddock fillets, frozen	500 g
1 lb	small red potatoes (unpeeled), about 4	500 g
4	green onions, chopped	4
1 cup	chopped celery	250 mL
Half	sweet red pepper, cut in chunks	Half

	Green or red-tipped leaf lettuce	
Mango Mayonnaise Dressing:		
1 cup	mayonnaise	250 mL
¼ cup	mango chutney	50 mL
1 tbsp	good-quality curry powder	15 mL
½ tsp	salt	2 mL

If using perch, remove skin by making small cut at narrowest end of partially thawed fillets; grasp skin tightly and pull off toward wide end. Cut fillets into 1½-inch (4 cm) pieces; poach frozen fish for 5 to 7 minutes or until fish flakes with fork. (See page 10 for poaching technique.) Drain well and set aside to let cool.

Scrub potatoes; cut into approximately 1½-inch (4 cm) pieces. Cook in boiling salted water until just tender; drain. In bowl, combine potatoes, onions, celery and red pepper; set aside.

Mango Mayonnaise Dressing: In small bowl, stir together mayonnaise, chutney, curry powder and salt. Pour over vegetables and toss to coat. Add cooked fish and gently toss. Cover and refrigerate for at least 1 hour for flavors to develop or up to 6 hours. At serving time, arrange lettuce on shallow serving dish; spoon salad on top.

Makes 4 to 6 servings.

GRILLED FISH SALAD WITH
TOMATO-THYME VINAIGRETTE

Simple but attractive, this warm salad combines the appealing flavors of smoky grilled fish and a refreshing tomato dressing. The fish will barbecue better if not completely thawed.

	Leaf, Boston or Romaine lettuce or combination			Sprigs fresh thyme (optional)	
				Tomato-Thyme Vinaigrette:	
1	stalk celery, thinly sliced	1	2 tbsp	white wine vinegar	25 mL
			½ tsp	Dijon mustard	2 mL
Half	red onion, thinly sliced	Half	½ tsp	minced fresh thyme (or pinch dried)	2 mL
4 tsp	coarsely chopped fresh thyme (or ½ tsp/2 mL dried)	20 mL	¼ tsp	freshly ground black pepper	1 mL
1 lb	cod fillets, partially thawed	500 g	Pinch	each granulated sugar and cayenne	Pinch
	Vegetable oil		¼ cup	vegetable oil	50 mL
1	tomato, cut in wedges	1	1	tomato	1

Tomato-Thyme Vinaigrette: In small bowl, whisk together vinegar, mustard, thyme, black pepper, sugar and cayenne. Whisk in oil. Set aside. In another bowl, chop to fine purée peeled, seeded tomato. (Recipe can be prepared to this point, covered and refrigerated overnight.) Whisk tomato purée into vinegar mixture.

Salad: Arrange lettuce on 4 dinner plates; sprinkle each evenly with celery, onion and thyme. Set aside.

Pat fillets dry with paper towels; brush all over with oil. Grill on well-greased grill over medium-hot coals or at medium setting for 4 to 8 minutes or until fish starts to flake with fork, turning only thicker fillets. Cut each fillet into about 3 strips and arrange evenly on top of lettuce-lined plates. Drizzle each with some of the Tomato-Thyme Vinaigrette. Garnish each plate with tomato wedges, and thyme sprigs if desired.

Makes 4 servings.

Fish contains vitamins A, B$_{12}$ and C, as well as thiamine, riboflavin, pyridoxine, niacin, folic acid and panothenic acid.

All fish are also good sources of phosphorous, iodine, copper and fluorine. In fact, fish has a slightly higher mineral content than meat, but is low in sodium.

FISH SALAD CRÉCY

Fish and carrots are always good partners. Here, raw grated carrots are marinated in the same vinaigrette that gives the fish an interesting flavor. When the two are combined in a simple composed salad, you have just the right main course for a steamy summer evening. Instead of cucumber and radish slices, nasturtium leaves and flowers make a wonderful edible garnish if you're lucky enough to have them at hand. (Back cover photograph.)

¼ cup	olive oil	50 mL	4	large carrots, finely grated (about 3½ cups/875 mL)	4
3 tbsp	lemon juice	50 mL			
2	cloves garlic, minced	2			
1 tbsp	finely chopped fresh thyme (or 1 tsp/5 mL dried)	15 mL	1 tbsp	drained capers	15 mL
			2	green onions, chopped	2
½ tsp	Dijon mustard	2 mL	Half	cucumber (unpeeled)	Half
	Salt and white pepper		4	large radishes, sliced	4
1	pkg (280 g) cod fillets, frozen	1			

In small bowl, whisk together oil, lemon juice, garlic, thyme, mustard, and salt and pepper to taste. Set aside. Poach fish for about 7 minutes or until fish flakes with fork (see page 10 for poaching technique).

Break into large flakes; place in medium bowl. While fish is still hot, pour in half of the vinaigrette; toss to coat. Cover and refrigerate for 30 minutes.

In large bowl, combine carrots, capers, green onions and remaining vinaigrette; toss to coat well. Cover and refrigerate for 30 minutes.

Just before serving, mound carrots on large platter; make indentation in centre and spoon in fish. Slice cucumber thinly; arrange around carrots. Place radish slices on top of cucumber.

Makes 3 or 4 servings.

A recipe for fish baked in ashes: No cheese, no nonsense! Just place it tenderly in fig leaves and tie them on top with a string: then push it under hot ashes, bethinking thee wisely of the time when it is done, and burn it not up.
Archestratus, Gastrology, 4th Century B.C.

GREEK GARDEN SALAD WITH GRILLED FISH

Enjoy this refreshing and colorful salad for lunch or a light supper with crusty bread. Serve on individual dinner plates or in a salad bowl.

1	pkg (280 g) cod fillets, thawed	1
4 cups	torn romaine lettuce	1 L
1	small red onion, thinly sliced	1
Half	large cucumber, quartered lengthwise, seeded and thickly sliced	Half
2	tomatoes, cut in thin wedges	2
¼ lb	feta cheese, cut in ½-inch (1 cm) cubes	125 g
½ cup	pitted black olives	125 mL
Dressing:		
½ cup	olive oil	125 mL
¼ cup	lemon juice	50 mL
1 tsp	Dijon mustard	5 mL
2	cloves garlic, minced	2
1 tsp	dried oregano	5 mL
Pinch	pepper	Pinch

Dressing: In small bowl, whisk together oil, lemon juice, mustard, garlic, oregano and pepper.

Salad: Pat fish dry with paper towels; place in shallow dish just big enough to hold fillets in single layer. Pour one-third of the dressing over top; cover and refrigerate for 1 hour. Set remaining dressing aside.

Just before serving, toss together lettuce, onion, cucumber, tomatoes, cheese and olives in large salad bowl. Stir remaining dressing and pour over salad; toss to coat. Place fish on well-oiled grill over medium-hot coals or at medium setting; grill fillets without turning, brushing with marinade, for about 5 minutes or until fish flakes with fork. (Alternatively, broil 3 inches/8 cm from heat for about 5 minutes.) Arrange hot fish on top of salad mixture.

Makes 4 servings.

TOASTED FISH AND TOMATO
SANDWICHES

BLTs become FLTs in these delicious sandwiches — perfect for lunch when tomatoes are at their harvest best. Teenagers might enjoy the fish in hamburger buns as "fishburgers."

Tapenade Mayonnaise (page 83) dresses up these simple sandwiches with an interesting flavor, but you could use plain mayonnaise.

1	pkg (280 g) fish fillets, thawed	1	8	slices French or Italian bread, toasted (or 4 kaiser rolls, split and toasted)	8
¼ cup	cornstarch	50 mL			
½ tsp	salt	2 mL			
¼ tsp	pepper	1 mL	2	tomatoes, thickly sliced	2
¼ tsp	paprika	1 mL			
2 tbsp	butter	25 mL		Salt and pepper	
1 tbsp	vegetable oil	15 mL		Leaf lettuce or coarsely shredded iceberg lettuce	
	Tapenade Mayonnaise (page 83)				

If necessary, cut fish into pieces that fit bread slices or buns. Pat fish dry with paper towels. On waxed paper or in shallow bowl, stir together cornstarch, salt, pepper and paprika. Dredge fish in mixture to coat well. If time permits, set aside for 30 minutes or refrigerate for up to 1 hour.

In large skillet, heat butter with oil over medium-high heat. Shake excess cornstarch mixture from fillets. Cook fish for about 3 minutes per side or until golden and fish flakes with fork.

Meanwhile, spread some of the Tapenade Mayonnaise generously over hot toast. Top 4 of the slices with fish and tomato slices; sprinkle with salt and pepper to taste. Top each with lettuce, then remaining slice of toast. Cut diagonally and serve immediately.

Makes 4 servings.

JAZZ IT UP

Sauces and butters are an easy way to add zest to simply broiled, poached, grilled, pan-fried or baked fish. And it's an easy way to add to your repertoire of fish recipes.

Remember there are other simple ways to jazz up plain fish. A drizzle of lemon juice or malt vinegar brings out its good flavor, but don't forget to try more unusual enhancers such as balsamic vinegar, orange or lime juice, and extra-virgin olive oil for distinctive flavor. Using juices, vinegars and herbs as seasonings instead of butters and oil cuts out calories too.

TARTAR SAUCE

This homemade tartar sauce goes particularly well with breaded or battered deep-fried fish.

1	egg	1	2 tbsp	finely chopped dill pickle	25 mL
2 tbsp	lemon juice	25 mL	1 tbsp	finely chopped pimiento	15 mL
½ tsp	Dijon mustard	2 mL			
¼ tsp	salt	1 mL	1 tbsp	drained capers	15 mL
Pinch	granulated sugar	Pinch	1 tbsp	finely chopped fresh parsley	15 mL
	White pepper				
¾ cup	vegetable oil	175 mL			

In blender or food processor, combine egg, lemon juice, mustard, salt, sugar, and pepper to taste. With motor running, add oil a few drops at a time through lid or feed tube until mixture starts to thicken; then add remaining oil in slow steady stream until all is absorbed. Blend in pimiento, capers and parsley. Transfer mixture to small bowl; cover and refrigerate for up to 5 days.

Makes 1 cup (250 mL).

RAITA SAUCE

Fresh coriander, also called cilantro or Chinese parsley, available at Chinese or other international grocery stores, adds an interesting touch to this delicious sauce. Serve the raita with any grilled, broiled or fried fish. It's especially good with Sole Waves (page 14).

1 cup	plain yogurt	250 mL		¼ tsp	dried orange rind (optional)	1 mL
½ cup	sour cream	125 mL		Pinch	each turmeric, white pepper and cayenne pepper	Pinch
⅔ cup	grated, seeded, peeled cucumber	150 mL				
1 tbsp	chopped fresh coriander	15 mL				
½ tsp	each salt, granulated sugar and curry powder	2 mL				

In medium bowl, stir together yogurt, sour cream, cucumber, coriander, salt, sugar, curry powder, orange rind (if using), turmeric, white pepper and cayenne pepper. Refrigerate, covered, for about 30 minutes for flavors to develop or for up to 2 days.

Makes about 2 cups (500 mL).

Herbs and Sauces Make Seafood Sensational

• Seafood has a delicate flavor so herbs, spices and sauces should not overpower its delicious flavor.

• Thyme, tarragon, savory, paprika, ginger, fennel, dill, curry powder, chervil and basil all add subtle flavor to seafood.

• 1 tbsp (15 mL) chardonnay or dry vermouth in the pan while you pan-fry fillets brings out the good flavor of fish and helps eliminate any odor.

QUICK HOMEMADE MAYONNAISE

Use a good prepared mayonnaise for the Mayonnaise Sauces (next page) or make this easy homemade one. Be sure all the ingredients and equipment are at room temperature and add the oil very, very gradually to ensure success.

1	large egg	1	
1 tsp	Dijon mustard	5 mL	
¼ tsp	salt	1 mL	
Pinch	each cayenne pepper and granulated sugar	Pinch	

1 tbsp	vinegar or lemon juice	15 mL
1 cup	good-quality vegetable oil, olive oil or a combination	250 mL

In blender or food processor, place egg, mustard, salt, cayenne, sugar and vinegar; blend for 4 seconds. With motor running on slowest speed, gradually add oil drop by drop, then increase to tiny, slow stream and process until thickened. Taste and adjust seasoning. Mayonnaise will keep covered and refrigerated for up to 2 weeks.

Makes 1½ cups (375 mL).

MAYONNAISE SAUCES

Mayonnaise-based sauces are not only easy to make but are also perfect accompaniments to hot *or* cold grilled, baked, pan-fried or poached fish.

Basil Mayonnaise

½ cup	mayonnaise	125 mL
2 tbsp	chopped fresh basil leaves	25 mL
1	small clove garlic, minced	1
Pinch	each salt, pepper and paprika	Pinch

In small bowl, stir together mayonnaise, basil, garlic, salt, pepper and paprika.

Makes about ½ cup (125 mL).

Horseradish Mayonnaise

½ cup	mayonnaise	125 mL
2 tbsp	drained prepared horseradish	25 mL
4 tsp	minced fresh parsley	20 mL

In small bowl, mix together mayonnaise, horseradish and parsley.

Makes about ¾ cup (175 mL).

Mustard Mayonnaise

½ cup	mayonnaise	125 mL
½ cup	Dijon mustard	125 mL

In small bowl, mix together mayonnaise and mustard.

Makes 1 cup (250 mL).

Lemon-dill Mayonnaise

½ cup	mayonnaise	125 mL
2 tbsp	plain yogurt or sour cream	25 mL
4 tsp	snipped fresh dill (or 1 tsp/5 mL dried dillweed)	20 mL
2 tsp	lemon juice	10 mL
¼ tsp	grated lemon rind	1 mL
¼ tsp	white pepper	1 mL

In small bowl, mix together mayonnaise, yogurt, dill, lemon juice, lemon rind and pepper.

Makes about ⅔ cup (150 mL).

Tapenade Mayonnaise

½ cup	mayonnaise	125 mL
2 tbsp	finely chopped pitted black olives	25 mL
2 tbsp	coarsely chopped drained capers	25 mL
½ tsp	anchovy paste	2 mL
1	small clove garlic, minced	1
Dash	hot pepper sauce	Dash

In small bowl, stir together mayonnaise, olives, capers, anchovy paste, garlic and hot pepper sauce. Cover and refrigerate for 30 minutes for flavors to blend.

Makes about ¾ cup (175 mL).

Garlic Mayonnaise (Aioli)

½ cup	mayonnaise	125 mL
4	cloves garlic, crushed	4

In small bowl, mix together mayonnaise and garlic.

Makes ½ cup (125 mL).

If making Quick Homemade Garlic Mayonnaise, drop 8 cloves garlic through feed tube and purée before adding egg to blender and continuing with recipe.

Makes 1 cup (250 mL).

Roasted Garlic Mayonnaise

10	large cloves garlic (unpeeled)	10
½ cup	mayonnaise	125 mL

Pierce each garlic clove; roast in 375°F (190°C) oven for 15 to 20 minutes or until soft. Let cool; press out garlic and mash smoothly. Blend into mayonnaise. Store up to 3 days in airtight container in refrigerator.

Makes ½ cup (125 mL).

Fish, to taste right, must swim three times — in water, in butter, and in wine.
Polish proverb

FLAVORED BUTTERS

Flavored, or compound, butters are an easy way to flavor fish. Roll the butter in waxed paper into cylinder shape and refrigerate until cold, then slice a flavorful 'coin' to melt on top of grilled or broiled fish. Or spread soft, flavored butter over fillets before baking or microwaving.

For easy mixing, have the butter at room temperature and cream the remaining ingredients in with a wooden spoon. Or combine everything in a food processor until smooth. If using a machine, use cold butter, cut into bits.

Lemon-parsley Butter
To ½ cup (125 mL) butter, add 2 tbsp (25 mL) chopped fresh parsley; 1 minced small clove garlic; ½ tsp (2 mL) grated lemon rind, 1 tsp (5 mL) lemon juice; and salt and pepper to taste.

Lemon-dill Butter
To ½ cup (125 mL) butter, add 2 tbsp (25 mL) snipped fresh dill (or 1 tsp/5 mL dried dillweed); 1 tbsp (15 mL) lemon juice; and salt and white pepper to taste.

Anchovy Butter
To ½ cup (125 mL) butter, add 1 tbsp (15 mL) anchovy paste (available in delicatessens); 1 minced small clove garlic; 1 tbsp (15 mL) finely chopped fresh thyme (or 1 tsp/5 mL crushed dried); and pinch pepper.

Lime-ginger Butter
To ½ cup (125 mL) butter, add 2 tbsp (25 mL) finely grated fresh gingerroot; 4 tsp (20 mL) fresh lime juice; ½ tsp (2 mL) grated lime rind; and pinch salt.

Mustard-chive Butter
To ½ cup (125 mL) butter, add 2 tbsp (25 mL) Dijon mustard; 2 tbsp (25 mL) snipped chives; and pepper to taste.

THOUSAND ISLAND SAUCE

Serve this refreshing sauce with any fried, baked or broiled fillets.

1 cup	mayonnaise	250 mL	1 tsp	minced pimiento	5 mL
¼ cup	tomato chili sauce	50 mL	½ tsp	grated lemon rind	2 mL
1 tbsp	minced sweet green pepper	15 mL	½ tsp	Worcestershire sauce	2 mL
1 tbsp	finely chopped green onion	15 mL			

In small bowl, stir together mayonnaise, chili sauce, green pepper, green onion, pimiento, lemon rind and Worcester shire sauce. (Sauce can be made ahead, covered and refrigerated for up to 1 week.)

Makes about 1½ cups (375 mL).

FRESH TOMATO SALSA

This quick uncooked tomato sauce is delicious over barbecued or broiled fish. Diced yellow sweet peppers can be added for additional colour as in the photograph opposite page 65.

1	tomato, peeled, seeded and diced	1	1 tbsp	lime juice	15 mL
¼ cup	diced red onion	50 mL	Pinch	granulated sugar	Pinch
1 tbsp	chopped fresh coriander	15 mL		Salt and pepper	
1 tbsp	minced fresh or canned jalapeño pepper	15 mL			

In small bowl, stir together tomato, onion, coriander, jalapeño pepper, lime juice, sugar, and salt and pepper to taste. Cover and refrigerate until serving time, up to 8 hours.

Makes about 1 cup (250 mL).

P Poached cod seem to bring out the finest nuances of flavor in an assortment of sauces including mayonnaise, hollandaise, Mornay and their derivatives.
Craig Claiborne's Favorites from The New York Times, Craig Claiborne, Times Books, 1976.

LIGHT HOLLANDAISE SAUCE

This light version of the classic sauce contains no butter, but gets lots of flavor from fresh lemon juice, a natural with fish.

3	eggs	3	¼ tsp	white pepper	1 mL
3 tbsp	lemon juice	45 mL	Dash	hot pepper sauce	Dash
¼ cup	hot water	50 mL			

In large bowl, whisk together eggs, lemon juice and hot water. Place over pan of hot, not boiling, water and whisk until fluffy and thickened, 3 to 4 minutes. Whisk in pepper and hot pepper sauce; cover and keep warm over hot water for up to 30 minutes. Taste and adjust seasoning.

Makes about ¾ cup (175 mL).

QUICK HOLLANDAISE SAUCE

This easy, buttery sauce is great on any poached, broiled or baked fish. It is especially delicious with Herb-stuffed Fillets Baked in Pastry (page 64).

3	egg yolks	3	Pinch	cayenne	Pinch
2 tbsp	lemon juice	25 mL	½ cup	sizzling-hot melted	125 mL
Pinch	each salt and pepper	Pinch		butter	

In blender or food processor, blend egg yolks, lemon juice, salt, pepper and cayenne for 30 seconds. With machine running, pour in sizzling butter in slow, steady stream. When mixture thickens, turn off machine and immediately pour into warmed serving bowl. (If making a few minutes ahead, pour into preheated Thermos.) Taste and adjust seasoning to serve.

Makes about ¾ cup (175 mL).

ROASTED RED PEPPER SAUCE WITH GARLIC

Charred red peppers and a dash of hot pepper sauce give this red-orange sauce (an adaptation of the classic rouille) an interesting depth of flavor with a fiery finish. Pour over grilled or broiled fish or drizzle on top of a steaming bowl of fish soup.

1	sweet red pepper (about 6 oz/175 g)	1	¼ cup	olive oil	50 mL
½ cup	firmly packed fresh bread crumbs	125 mL	¼ tsp	paprika	1 mL
3	cloves garlic	3	Dash	hot pepper sauce	Dash
			Pinch	each salt and pepper	Pinch

Broil red pepper about 4 inches (10 cm) from heat for 4 minutes per side or until skin browns and blisters. Place in saucepan, cover and steam for 10 minutes. Peel away charred skin, seed and remove membranes. Chop coarsely and pat dry with paper towels.

Meanwhile, soak bread crumbs in water. Drain through sieve, pressing firmly to remove moisture.

In food processor or blender with motor running, drop garlic and process until finely chopped. Add roasted pepper and bread crumbs; process until smooth, stopping to scrape down sides. With motor running, gradually pour in oil; process until thickened and sauce has consistency of light mayonnaise. Blend in paprika, hot pepper sauce, salt and pepper. Taste and adjust seasoning. Serve immediately or cover and refrigerate for up to 2 days. If refrigerated, bring to room temperature.

Makes ¾ cup (175 mL).

CREAM SAUCE

Layer flaked poached fish, cooked pasta, grated Parmesan cheese and steamed broccoli with this simple sauce for a quick and delicious supper.

2 tbsp	butter	25 mL	Herbs or other
2 tbsp	all-purpose flour	25 mL	seasonings such as
1 cup	hot milk	250 mL	nutmeg or cayenne
	Salt and pepper		pepper as desired

In heavy saucepan, melt butter. Add flour and cook over low heat, stirring, for 2 minutes. Do not brown. Remove from heat and whisk in hot milk, salt and pepper to taste and seasonings.

Increase heat to medium and cook, stirring, for 1 to 2 minutes, or until sauce is thickened and smooth. Taste and adjust seasoning.

Makes 1 cup (250 mL).

VARIATIONS:

Cheese Sauce

Add ¼ to 1 cup (50 to 250 mL) coarsely shredded Cheddar or Swiss cheese to hot thickened sauce; stir until melted.

Egg Sauce

Add 2 chopped hard-cooked eggs and 1 tbsp (15 mL) each lemon juice and minced fresh parsley to hot thickened sauce.

Microwave Method

In 4-cup (1 L) glass measure, microwave butter at High for 1 minute or until melted. Stir in flour and microwave at High for 30 seconds. Gradually stir in milk to blend well. Microwave at High for 3 to 3½ minutes, stirring every minute, or until sauce is bubbly and thickened.

PESTO SAUCE

This fresh basil sauce goes well with poached, grilled, baked or pan-fried fillets. It also makes an interesting addition to fish soup if you spread the pesto on toasted French bread to float on top.

2 cups	packed fresh basil leaves	500 mL	½ tsp	(approx) salt	2 mL
			¼ tsp	pepper	1 mL
½ cup	olive oil	125 mL	½ cup	freshly grated Parmesan cheese	125 mL
¼ cup	pine nuts or chopped walnuts	50 mL			
3	large cloves garlic	3	2 tbsp	butter (optional)	25 mL

In food processor or blender, combine basil, oil, nuts, garlic, salt and pepper; purée and transfer to medium bowl. Stir in cheese. Taste and add more salt if desired. Cover and refrigerate in airtight container for up to 3 days or freeze for up to 3 months. If you wish, blend in butter just before using.

Makes 1 cup (250 mL).

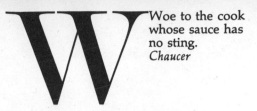

W Woe to the cook whose sauce has no sting.
Chaucer

CREOLE SAUCE

Serve this easy cooked tomato sauce with Cod Cakes (page 45), or any broiled or pan-fried fillets. It's especially good when pooled on a platter, then topped with ocean perch fillets which have been dusted in cornmeal and pan-fried in butter.

1 tbsp	butter	15 mL		½ cup	chicken stock	125 mL
1	onion, coarsely chopped	1		1 tbsp	paprika	15 mL
				1	bay leaf	1
1	sweet green pepper, coarsely chopped	1		¼ tsp	granulated sugar	1 mL
					Salt and pepper	
1	stalk celery, coarsely chopped	1			Hot pepper sauce	
				2 tbsp	minced fresh parsley	25 mL
1	clove garlic, minced	1				
1	can (14 oz/398 mL) tomatoes (undrained), chopped	1				

In medium saucepan, heat butter over medium heat; cook onion, green pepper and celery for 5 minutes. Stir in garlic and cook for a few seconds. Stir in tomatoes, stock, paprika, bay leaf, sugar, salt (if necessary), pepper and 2 or 3 dashes hot pepper sauce to taste. Bring to boil; reduce heat to medium-low and simmer, uncovered, for about 10 minutes or until thickened. Remove bay leaf and stir in parsley. (Sauce can be prepared ahead, cooled, covered and refrigerated up to 5 days or frozen up to 2 months.) Serve hot.

Makes 2 cups (500 mL).

SEAFOOD GLOSSARY

CHOWDER: a thick milk or tomato-based soup made with seafood and vegetables, especially potatoes and carrots.

DEEP FRY: to cook immersed in hot oil.

FILLET (phil - IT): a side section of fish which has been cut away from the backbone — usually the skin and bones have been removed; also the act of removing a fillet from a fish.

FLAKE: describes the texture of the flesh of cooked fish when broken into pieces with a fork.

OVEN-FRY: to cook in the oven using less fat than in pan-frying.

OVEN-STEAM: to cook in the oven wrapped in foil or parchment paper.

PAN-FRY: to cook on top of the stove over medium-low to medium heat.

POACH: to cook below the boiling point in a simmering liquid such as water, milk or wine.

POLYUNSATURATED FAT: one of the 3 types of fatty acids found in fats; polyunsaturated fats, which lower the level of cholesterol in blood, are found in seafood; certain highly polyunsaturated fatty acids called Omega-3 occur exclusively in seafood and marine animals.

SAUTÉE: to cook on top of the stove over medium heat.

SEVICHE: fish or shellfish marinated in citrus juice; the acid in the juice breaks down the protein, thus "cooking" the raw fish.

STEAM: to cook or steam with or without pressure; steam may be applied directly to the seafood as in a steamer or a pressure cooker.

STIR-FRY: a form of sautéing, but over higher heat and usually in a wok.

Adapted from the *Canadian Seafood Education Kit.*

RECIPE INDEX